D0538645

PETÉN

MEXICO
MÉXICO
GUATEMALA

Guadalupe
Poptún
San Luis

TOLEDO
Casemero
Palma
Monkey River
RANGUANA CAY
Punta Negra
North Spot
SAPODILLA
CAYS

ISLA DE ROATÁN
Roatán
ISLAS DE

San Antonio
Punta Gorda
Port Honduras
Gulf of Honduras
ISLA DE UTILA
Utila

Mateo
Ixtatan
Barillas
Santa
Eulalia

Chisec

ALTA VERAPAZ

Chahal
Cahabón
San Juan
Livingston
Punta de
Amatique
Puerto Cortés
Bahía de Omoa
Baracoa
El Triunfo
Colorado
Corozal
La Ceiba
PUNTA IZOPO
PUNTA CATCHABUTAN

QUICHÉ
Chajul
Nebaj
San Juan Cotzal
2739

Lanquín
San Pedro Carchá
Senahú
Cobán
San Cristóbal
Verapaz
Panzos

SIERRA DE
SANTA CRUZ
Castillo de
San Felipe
El Estor
Lago de
Izabal
Izabal
1067
Puerto
Barrios
MONTAÑAS DEL MICO
Morales

Cuyamel
Choloma
Cofradía
Chamelecón
San Pedro Sula
La Lima
El Progreso
Tela
Cerro San
Ildefonso
ATLÁNTIDA
La Masica
Mezapa
Pico Bonito
2435
NOMBRE
Olanchito

Huehuetenango
San Andrés Sajcabajá
Chichicastenango
Santa Cruz del Quiché
BAJA VERAPAZ
Rabinal
Salamá
San
Jerónimo
3139
Gualán
ZACAPA
Zacapa
1716
Jocotán
Copán
COPÁN
Santa Rosa
de Copán
Naranjito
San José
Santa Bárbara
Las Vegas
2744
Azacualpa
San Marcos
Macuelizo
Potrerillos
Santa Rita
Cerro Cuchilla
Alta 1737
Pico Pijol
2282
Minas de Oro
La Libertad
San Ignacio
Cedros
Guarizama
Guayape
Orica
Salamá
Campamento

TOTONI-
CAPÁN
San Cristóbal
Totonicapán
SOLOLÁ
Sololá
Santa Cruz
CHIMALTENANGO
Tecpán Guatemala
IXIMCHÉ
Comalapa
Chimaltenango
EL PROGRESO
San Juan Sacatepéquez
San Pedro Ayampuc
El Progreso
2176
Jalapa
San Pedro Pinula
JALAPA
Esquipulas
CHIQUIMULA
Quezaltepeque
San Luis
Jilotepeque
Florida
Trinidad
Arada
Gracias
Cerro Azul
Taulabé
COMAYAGUA
Siguatepeque
Comayagua
San Antonio
YORO
Yoro
2164
Mangulile
Guaimaca
Monte Mucupina
Mo

Volcán Santa
Maria
3772
Santiago
Atitlán
Antigua
Guatemala
San Antonio
3537
Ciudad Vieja
Villa Nueva
Volcán
de Agua
3766
Palín
GUATEMALA
Guatemala
Escuintla
Barberena
El Progreso
Jutiapa
Asunción
Mita
Metapán
Nueva
Ocotepeque
San
Sebastián
La Palma
INTIBUCÁ
Intibucá
La Esperanza
Jesús de
Otoro
Cerro Las Minas
2849
2225
CORDILLERA
Ajuterique
La Paz
San Antonio
Márcala
2256
Villa de
San Francisco
FRANCISCO
MORAZÁN
Villa de
San Francisco
La Libertad

CHIMACHE
QUEZA
QUIX
Suchitepéquez
Retalhuleu
Santa Lucía
Cotzumalguapa
Masagua
ESCUINTLA
Guazacapán
Taxisco
Chiquimulilla
Volcán Tecuamburro
1840
Volcán Moyuta 1662
JUTIAPA
El Adelanto
Asunción
Mita
Chalchuapa
Ahuachapán
Atiquizaya
SANTA ROSA
Nueva
Concepción
Concepción
Quezaltepeque
Arcatao
Chalatenango
Aguilares
Nueva
Concepción
LEMPIRA
MONTAÑA
LA SIERRA
LA PAZ
2243
Yerba Buena
Tegucigalpa
EL PARAÍSO
Danlí
Yuscarán
Jacaleapa
El Paraíso
Pico
Mogot
2107

Barrita Vieja
Puerto de
San José
Buena Vista
Garita Palmera
Pasaco
Volcán de Santa
Ana 2365
Izalco
Nahuizalco
Sonsonate
Santa
Ana
El
Congo
SANTA ANA
Volcán Izalco 1960
Acajutla
PUNTA
REMEDIOS
Nueva San Salvador
San Salvador
San Marcos
La Libertad
Suchitoto
Quezaltepeque
Apopa
Soyapango
Villa
Delgado
Mejicanos
Cojutepeque
San
Vicente
Ilobasco
San Sebastián
Volcán de
San Vicente
2181
Carolina
Ciudad Barrios
Guatajiagua
Estanzuelas
Lolotique
San Francisco Gotera
Santa Rosa
de Lima
Corinto
Langue
Sabanagrande
Pespire
VALLE
Nacaome
CHOLUTECA
El Corpus
Cerro Rincón
del Ocote
1154
San Marcos
de Colón
Orocuina
Choluteca
Cerro Guanacaure
1020
El Triunfo
Somotillo
Villanueva
Ocotal
Somoto
Pueblo
Nuevo
ESTELÍ
San Juan
de Limay
Santo Tomás
de Nance
Condega
NUE
MAD
San José
de Achuapa
El Sauce
Cerro
1550

San Marcelino
Zacatecoluca
Jiquilisco
La Tasajera
Chinameca
San Jorge
Santa Elena
Usulután
Puerto
El Triunfo
Bahía de Jiquilisco
Chirilagua
El Cuco
San Rafael Oriente
El Transito
Jucuapa
San Miguel 2130
San Alejo
San Lorenzo
San Miguel
La Unión
Conchagua
Volcán de
Conchagua
1243
Amapala
ISLA EL
TIGRE
PUNTA
AMAPALA
Golfo de
Fonseca
Intipucá
Volcán
Conchagua
Jocoro
Cinco Pinos
PACIFIC

León
CORDILLERA
DE LOS
MARIBIOS
La Paz
Centro
Nagarote
Puerto
Somoza
Mana
Villa el Carmen
Diri
San Rafael del Sur
Masachapa
C.

Chinandega
Chichigalpa
Corinto
PUNTA CASTAÑONES
CHINANDEGA
El Viejo
Volcán San Cristóbal
1745
Volcán
Telica
1060
Volcán Cosigüina 859
Puerto Morazán
PUNTA
COSIGÜINA
Estero
Mina el
Limón
Larreynag
Malpaisillo
LEÓN
Volcán

▽ 6349
▽ 5137
▽ 3737
▽ 5322
▽ 5356
▽ 3529
▽ 3387
▽ 4014
▽ 2933
▽ 33
▽ 146
2061

Enchantment of the World

EL SALVADOR

By Faren Maree Bachelis

Consultant for El Salvador: George I. Blanksten, Ph.D., Professor Emeritus of Political Science, Northwestern University, Evanston, Illinois

Consultant for Reading: Robert L. Hillerich, Ph.D., Bowling Green State University, Bowling Green, Ohio

CHILDRENS PRESS®
CHICAGO

People in Cojutepeque on the way to the daily market

Library of Congress Cataloging-in-Publication Data

Bachelis, Faren Maree.
    El Salvador / by Faren Maree Bachelis.
        p.   cm. — (Enchantment of the world)
    Summary: Discusses the geography, history, politics,
people, and culture of this Central American nation.
    ISBN 0-516-02718-2
    1. El Salvador—Description and travel—1981—
Juvenile literature.   2. El Salvador—History—Juvenile
literature.   [1. El Salvador.] I. Title. II. Series.
F1484.3.B33   1990
972.8405'3—dc20   89-25419
                                                        CIP
                                                        AC

Picture Acknowledgments
AP/Wide World Photos, Inc.: 40 (2 photos), 44, 45 (left),
49 (2 photos), 53 (left), 55 (left), 57, 59, 61
© **Carlos Cordova, Ed.D.:** 10 (right), 41 (right), 48, 70
(center left), 73 (left), 74 (2 photos), 75 (2 photos), 77 (3
photos), 81 (right), 87 (left), 92 (right), 99, 105 (2 photos),
107, 110 (top left, bottom right)
The Marilyn Gartman Agency: 53 (right), 70 (top right)
© **Virginia Grimes:** 89 (right)
Historical Picture Service, Chicago: 29
North Wind Picture Archives: 26 (2 photos), 28 (2
photos), 37

© **Chip and Rosa Maria de la Cueva Peterson:** 4, 5, 6 (top),
12, 15, 16 (bottom right), 17, 20, 25, 30 (right), 41 (left), 43
(right), 69 (left), 86 (top), 90 (right), 102 (left), 104 (2
photos), 110 (top right, bottom left)
© **Photri:** 23, 69 (right), 70 (top left, bottom left), 85
(bottom left), 87 (right), 92 (left), 111; © **Lance Downing**,
16 (top right), 82 (top), 86 (bottom); © **Spillane**, 88 (left),
101
Root Resources: © **Roy Koz,** Cover, 8, 13, 85 (top left);
© **Michael Everett**, 6 (bottom), 70 (bottom right), 110
(center left)
Shostal Associates/SuperStock International, Inc.: 10
(left), 11, 22, 35 (left), 73 (right), 84 (right), 88 (right), 103
(2 photos); © **Eric Carle**, 16 (left), 30 (left), 35 (right), 82
(bottom), 84 (left), 85 (right); © **K. Kummels**, 67 (right), 89
(left)
© **Lynn Stone:** 19 (center)
Tom Stack & Associates: © Kevin Schafer, 19 (bottom
left); © **Bill Everitt**, 19 (right)
Tony Stone Worldwide-Click/Chicago: © Elizabeth
Harris, 70 (center right), 90 (left), 91 (right), 102 (right);
© **Sheryl McNee**, 108
SuperStock International, Inc.: 91 (left), 112
Third Coast Stock Source: © Janice L. Mahlberg, 81 (left)
UPI/Bettmann Newsphotos: 39, 43 (left), 45 (right), 47, 50
(2 photos), 55 (right), 62, 65 (2 photos), 78, 80, 95 (2
photos)
Valan: © **Bruce Lyon**, 19 (top left); © **Stephen J.
Krasemann**, 20 (inset); © **Anthony Scullion**, 67 (left)
Len W. Meents: Maps on pages 83, 87
**Courtesy Flag Research Center, Winchester,
Massachusetts 01890:** Flag on back cover
Cover: Lake Ilopango

This colorful display of produce in Zacatecoluca is typical of village markets in El Salvador.

TABLE OF CONTENTS

The upper class housing (above) in San Salvador, and the
shanty town (below) on the outskirts of the city, dramatically
illustrate the chasm between the two worlds of El Salvador.

Chapter 1

A LAND DIVIDED

In San Salvador, El Salvador, the wealthy live in lavish hilltop homes in rich residential districts. Below them lie ravines, lined with ramshackle cardboard, tin, and mud dwellings of the desperately poor. From patios surrounded by swimming pools and lush gardens, the rich can gaze across the top of the ravines at the city's expanse, oblivious of the misery beneath them.

This image powerfully illustrates the chasm between the two worlds in this tiny, crowded, and bitterly divided Central American nation: the world of the rich and middle class and the much larger world of the poor. This difference is rooted in the era when Spanish colonists imposed a feudal system upon all of Central America. Although the period of Spanish domination ended more than 150 years ago, the Spanish legacy remains.

El Salvador has the most unequal distribution of income in all of Latin America. As many as 70 percent of El Salvador's people are rural peasants (*campesinos*) mired in absolute poverty, as they have been for centuries. By contrast, a small elite owns most of the nation's land and wealth. A lack of democratic institutions and a system of fierce military rule have helped the wealthy to protect their power and privileged way of life. Although there have been some attempts to change the system, economic and political power remains firmly in the hands of the elite.

Coastal countryside near El Zonte

In the 1960s and 1970s, many Salvadoreans began to challenge the government. Unsuccessful attempts at peaceful change through elections, strikes, and mass protests led to armed insurrection. Since 1980, El Salvador has been racked by a violent and bloody civil war. More than seventy thousand people have been killed, most of them civilians. Thousands have been kidnapped and tortured or have simply disappeared. Any discussion of El Salvador is likely to be charged with emotion. Every aspect of the conflict is controversial.

This turmoil has overshadowed another side of El Salvador, which is far more than a country of controversy. Behind the newspaper headlines and television reports is a land of striking natural beauty and hardworking, friendly people. Although they remain deeply divided, all Salvadoreans share a fierce love for their beautiful land and undying loyalty toward their country.

Chapter 2

LAND OF VOLCANOES

El Salvador is a land of volcanoes. Dark and brooding, they dominate the landscape of this tiny nation nestled into the Pacific coast of Central America. Encompassing just 8,124 square miles (21,041 square kilometers), El Salvador is the smallest mainland nation of the Western Hemisphere. It is only 163 miles (262 kilometers) wide and 88 miles (142 kilometers) long, about the size of the state of Massachusetts or a little larger than Israel. The country borders Honduras on the north and east and Guatemala on the northwest. Nicaragua is to the southeast, across the Gulf of Fonseca.

More than twenty-five volcanoes rise above El Salvador's massive black lava fields, rolling grassland, sparkling blue lakes, and lush valleys. There are more volcanoes here than in any other Central American nation. Four are active—they still smolder, and from time to time erupt in dazzling plumes of red-hot lava. Many of the volcanoes are named for nearby towns and cities, such as Santa Ana, San Vicente, San Miguel, and San Salvador. Santa Ana Volcano is the country's tallest volcanic peak, rising to a height of about 7,800 feet (2,377 meters).

Izalco is El Salvador's newest volcano and one of its most famous. It stands in the western part of the country near the city

Izalco (left), which was formed in 1770, is El Salvador's newest volcano. For about two hundred years it erupted regularly. Today just a little smoke wafts from its cone. Right: Izalco erupting in 1957

for which it was named. One legend says that on February 23, 1770, villagers heard a loud rumbling like thunder from a rock in a field. The rumbling continued and the earth shook constantly. Then, a tremendous upheaval opened up the earth and a small hill formed. From its own spewing of molten lava and ash, the mountain eventually grew to more than 6,000 feet (1,829 meters). For two hundred years, Izalco erupted regularly every three to five minutes. At night the spewing flames and white-hot boulders could be seen from the sea. This earned it the nickname, "The Lighthouse of the Pacific."

Nine-tenths of the land was created by volcanoes, which play an important role in El Salvador's landscape and society. Due to all the volcanic activity, the soil is rich and porous with volcanic ash and lava, which makes it extremely fertile and productive. This rich soil is the nation's chief natural resource. It is ideal for growing coffee, the nation's largest crop.

A geothermal plant near Ahuachapan

Geysers and hot sulfur springs supply energy for much of the country. The heat from the water is used to produce electricity. Outcroppings of lava rock dot the countryside. Some are very large, such as the huge formation of black rock along the road between San Salvador and Santa Ana. Salvadoreans call it *El Mar de Lava* (The Sea of Lava).

The majesty of El Salvador's volcanic landscape has inspired the imagination of artists and poets. In his poem titled "El Maizal," Vicente Acosta wrote:

Below the heat of the tropics, the ancient forest
Intoxicated with light and life, seems to doze fitfully.
Filtering through it, the bright sun's golden shafts
Stain the ground with clear-cut shadows.
Above, the outline of volcanoes
Cuts into the steely stretch of sky.

11

San Vicente Volcano

LANDFORMS

Two rows of volcanoes run from east to west, dividing the country into three distinct regions. They are the coastal lowlands in the south, the central plateau, and the northern mountains. The countryside is diverse, ranging from tropical beaches to pine-covered mountains to rolling grasslands to dry semidesert. The landscape is striking with its dazzling color, brightly colored birds, reptiles, and monkeys, set off by abundant flowers and many shades of verdant trees and bushes.

12

A lovely cove on the Pacific shore

COASTAL LOWLANDS

The coastal lowlands occupy a narrow strip of fertile soil that extends ten to twenty miles (sixteen to thirty-two kilometers) inland from the Pacific Ocean. The region is a relatively flat plain, which stretches the length of the country from the Guatemalan border on the west to the Gulf of Fonseca on the east. This is the country's only coastline, which runs for 189 miles (304 kilometers) and is edged mostly by sandy beaches and dotted with bays, estuaries, capes, and islands. Beaches are sometimes broken by rocky points where ancient lava flows once poured into the sea. In some areas steep cliffs rise against a backdrop of rugged mountains and volcanoes.

Tropical forests, grasslands, and swamps once covered much of the region. Today most of the land has been developed for farming and industry. Most of the nation's cotton is grown here. A variety of tropical wildlife, such as tapirs, iguanas, and armadillos, live in the coastal lowlands. They may be found in the remaining grasslands and forests, where palm trees, mangoes, coconuts, and tamarinds grow profusely.

The coastal lowlands are the only area in El Salvador with tropical heat and humidity. Because the weather is warm all year round, with an average temperature of 80 degrees Fahrenheit (26.7 degrees Celsius), going to the beach is a popular outing. There are many beautiful beaches with sand ranging from pure white to volcanic black. Some have rough surf, while others are protected and tranquil. The most popular beach is at La Libertad, a port city about nineteen miles (thirty kilometers) south of San Salvador. Another favored beach is at Acajutla, the site of El Salvador's largest port. Much of El Salvador's commercial fishing industry is centered around this port, which has a mile-long pier for cargo ships.

The region between La Libertad and Acajutla is known as La Costa del Bálsamo. It is named for the trees that produce balsam sap, which has been used for centuries in the production of medicine and cosmetics. El Salvador is one of the few balsam producers in the world.

La Unión is an old port town on the Gulf of Fonseca, which separates El Salvador from Honduras and Nicaragua. Sheltered coves along the gulf were often used as hiding places by pirates during colonial times. One of the world's largest collections of native and migratory seabirds can be found on the gulf and its many islands.

The central plateau, on which San Salvador is located

CENTRAL PLATEAU

A row of volcanoes called the Coastal Range separates the coastal lowlands from the central plateau. This is the largest part of the country and includes most of its population, industry, and farming. El Salvador's three largest cities are located here. They are Santa Ana, San Miguel, and the capital city of San Salvador. Although the region also is known as the central valley, it is actually a plateau averaging some 2,000 feet (610 meters) in elevation. The weather is pleasant, with warm days and cool nights. The average annual temperature is 75 degrees Fahrenheit (23.9 degrees Celsius).

The rolling countryside is interspersed with mountains, volcanoes, and river valleys. Much of the forestland has been destroyed. Still, more than 10 percent of the landscape is covered with forests and woodland. Subtropical grassland covers most of the land, which is dotted with small trees and bushes such as

*Lake Ilopango (above) and Lake Coatepeque (above right)
both fill volcanic craters.
Right: Cattle grazing on a small ranch*

dogwood, mahogany, cedar, walnut, and rubber. Tropical fruit
and medicinal plants also grow here.

Lush valleys of rich soil are ideal for growing coffee and
sugarcane, another important Salvadorean crop. Coffee
plantations and cattle ranches are found among oak and pine
forests along the lower slopes of the Coastal Range.

El Salvador has more than three hundred lakes and rivers. The
two largest lakes are found in the central region, both filling
volcanic craters. The sapphire-blue Lake Ilopango, just east of San
Salvador, is subject to extreme high and low tides periodically. In
1880, the waters overflowed and then withdrew dramatically,
revealing a 150-foot (46-meter) island in the center of the lake.
South of Santa Ana and ringed by hills planted with coffee is Lake
Coatepeque, with hot springs and numerous green islands. The
lake is so deep that its bottom is yet to be found.

An aerial view of Río Lempa, the nation's largest river

The Río Lempa is the nation's largest river and its major source of hydroelectric power. It rises in Guatemala and runs for 160 miles (257 kilometers) in a sideways S shape through the country. River shrimp, called *camarones del río*, live in the waters where rivers meet the sea. They are large (about the size of a tiny lobster) and have a slightly sweet taste. Colorful fish, turtles, crocodiles, and alligators live in the network of rivers and streams, none of which are navigable by large boats.

NORTHERN MOUNTAINS

The northern region is formed by the Sierra Madre, the northern east-west mountain range that extends to the Honduran border. This area is sparsely populated, with several towns, small farms, and ranches. The land is mostly dry and semi-barren, made up primarily of lava rock and volcanic ash. There once were many forests here, but they too disappeared with overexploitation. The nation's coolest temperatures are found in this region, which receives the least amount of rain. The climate is mostly warm along the Lempa River valley and mild on the upper mountain slopes.

CLIMATE

El Salvador has a pleasantly warm climate. Temperatures vary generally with altitude, although there are no extremes of hot and cold. El Salvador has only two distinct seasons, rainy and dry. The rainy season, known as *invierno* (winter), lasts from May to October. The dry season, known as *verano* (summer), runs from November to April. The song of the *guace* bird announces the beginning and end of the rainy season. The mornings are sunny and dry, with rains coming every afternoon or evening. Clearing as quickly as they come, the rains leave behind brilliant blue skies and fluffy white clouds. Longer downpours, called *temporales*, sometimes occur during July and August. They may last for two or three days and can cause serious flooding. Some 80 inches (203 centimeters) of rain fall during this season, when the countryside becomes intensely green.

ANIMALS

Because so much of El Salvador's land is used for farming and pasture, few large predatory animals remain. Jaguars, ocelots, and pumas, all members of the cat family, still live in wilderness areas. Coyotes may be found also, along with a large variety of smaller

Clockwise from bottom left:
A jaguar,
a morpho butterfly,
a scarlet macaw,
and a marmoset

animals, such as rodents, reptiles, birds, and insects. Salvadoreans are treated to thousands of varieties of colorful butterflies. Many species of monkey, including the spider monkey, the marmoset, and the white-throated capuchin, live in the country's remaining thickly wooded areas.

There is a variety of birds, from white owls, black vultures, and hawks to waterfowl, such as pelicans, herons, swans, ducks, and geese. More than thirty-four species of colorful parrots perch in the treetops, including brightly colored red- and blue-headed macaws and parakeets. Many of El Salvador's birds are migratory. They arrive from the north in September or October for the winter, then leave in March or April. Many of the birds known to North Americans also were favorites of the Maya. The hummingbird is called *tzunuum*; the cardinal, *co-pol-che*; and the red-winged blackbird, *chuleb*.

The fertile volcanic soil (below) and the rich variety of plant and animal life attracted the early inhabitants of the area that is now called El Salvador. Right: A banana blossom is one of the many exotic flowers that grow there.

Chapter 3

FROM INDIAN LAND
TO SPANISH COLONY

Much of modern El Salvador's cultural and physical landscape has evolved from a blend of native Indian and Spanish colonial people and customs. For thousands of years before the Spanish arrived, El Salvador was an Indian land. Many different people settled here, attracted by the fertile volcanic soil, the favorable climate, and the rich variety of plant and animal life.

As many as half a million Indians may have inhabited El Salvador by the early sixteenth century. Today, less than 10 percent of its people are full-blooded Indian.

AN INDIAN LAND

Most of what is known about Central America's earliest inhabitants comes from archaeologists. Earthquakes and volcanic eruptions in El Salvador have left the remains of the early cultures in sometimes unsystematic relationships to each other.

Among the first people known to live in the region now called El Salvador were the Nahua Indians, a nomadic people long

Mayan architects built imposing temples.

established in Mexico. Over time, they learned to cultivate corn (maize) and other crops. This enabled them to remain in one area to build villages. By 2000 B.C., the Nahua were living in small farming communities.

Remains of several advanced pre-Columbian (before European contact) civilizations have been found in the western region of El Salvador. The oldest is the Olmec, a highly developed farming society that arose in eastern Mexico by about 1500 B.C. They built large ceremonial centers, pyramids, and huge stone sculptures. The most famous of these are the great stone heads weighing more than 20 tons (18,144 kilograms). One such head was found near the town of Chalchuapa, evidence of the Olmec's presence in El Salvador. Called the Olmec Boulder, its sides are carved in bas-relief and show figures of fierce warriors with jaguar heads.

THE MAYA

The Olmec were followed by the Maya, a highly advanced civilization that flourished from A.D. 300 to 900. Their empire

Mayan ruins at Tazumal, one of the country's most important archaeological sites

covered all of Guatemala and Belize and parts of Mexico, El Salvador, and Honduras. The Maya were known as great architects and engineers, building elaborate cities, excellent roads, and imposing temples. They developed a written language and were accomplished sculptors and artists. The Maya were especially brilliant mathematicians and astronomers.

The driving force behind all of their achievements was a complex religion based on corn, the Maya staff of life. If the corn grew, everyone ate; if it did not, everyone starved. It was believed to be a sacred plant, given to humans by the gods. Special prayers were made during sowing and harvesting of corn, which the Maya addressed as ''Your Grace.''

Although El Salvador was never a center of Mayan culture, ruins in the western region attest to their influence. Stepped pyramid temples, paved plazas, and ball courts are found at sites such as El Trapito, San Andrés, and Tazumal, the country's most important archaeological site yet excavated.

THE PIPIL

As the influence of the Maya declined, the Pipil Indians came to dominate the region west of the Lempa River. The Pipil were descendants of Nahua-speaking Toltecs, and later the Aztecs, both of Mexico. It is believed that they came from Mexico to found the Pipil nation in the eleventh century, although other groups of Nahua-speakers had been in El Salvador since before the Maya. The name *Pipil*, which means "language of children," was given to them later by the Aztecs who accompanied the Spanish conquerors. The Aztecs recognized that the Pipil spoke the same language, but felt they mispronounced it as children might.

The Pipil named the land Cuscatlán, meaning "land of precious things." They developed an advanced culture, similar to that of the Aztecs, but with a large Mayan influence. A complex social system included nobility, priests, artisans, and warriors. Although primarily an agricultural people, they built large cities and developed hieroglyphic writing, mathematics, and astronomy. Artisans created distinctive pottery, stone carvings, and gold and silver ornaments.

The nation was divided into seven chiefdoms, each ruled separately by a local chief. The largest was Cuscatlán, located southeast of present-day San Salvador, which had a population of perhaps ten thousand. Its ruling elite dominated all the others. The second-most important chiefdom was Izalco. Many present-day Indians are found in the township of Izalco.

Families were grouped in clans called *calpulli*, led by a local chief, and given a plot of land to farm but not to own. All lands were communal, because the Indians believed people could no more own the land than they could own the sky, sea, or weather.

Corn is as important today as it was to the earlier civilizations of El Salvador.

The importance of the *milpa* (cornfield) for Salvadorean peasants today is rooted in the tradition and culture of the Maya and Pipil. The staple crop of the Pipil was corn, as it had been with the Maya. Corn formed the basis of their culture and religion. Because survival depended upon their crops, they worshiped the gods of corn, sun, rain, wind, earth, and fire. The Indians believed the gods were in each plant, so to eat the plant was to share communion with the source of being.

The Pipil also grew beans, cacao (cocoa), cotton, squash, chili peppers, and tobacco, and produced honey and wax. Farmers used fire to clear the milpa and sharpened sticks to dig and plant. The work was difficult and time-consuming, as they did not have plows, wheels, or draft animals.

Warfare was common among the various chiefdoms and between other Indian groups who occupied the territory. The largest of these was the Lenca, who settled north and east of the Lempa River. Their kingdom was called Chaparrestique and the ruins of their chief center are near present-day San Miguel.

Hernán Cortés

Pedro de Alvarado

SPANISH CONQUEST AND COLONIZATION

The Indian world was disrupted and changed forever with the
arrival of the Spanish early in the sixteenth century. Led by
Hernán Cortés, gold-hungry conquistadores began their conquest
of Latin America, eventually winning one of the world's greatest
empires for Spain. After conquering Mexico in 1519, Cortés turned
his attention south. Rumors of riches in the isthmus led him to
send Pedro de Alvarado, one of his principal lieutenants, to bring
the region into the Spanish realm.

After conquering Guatemala, Alvarado and his army reached
the Pacific coast near the present-day Salvadorean port of Acajutla
in June 1524. Clad in armor, steel blade in mailed fist, the tall, red-
bearded Alvarado and his mounted troops must have inspired
awe in the eyes of the Indians. They had never before seen horses,
and thought the horse and man were one creature, perhaps even a
god. Gods or not, the intruders posed a serious threat to the Pipil,
whose warriors bitterly resisted the invasion. Alvarado ordered
the massacre of the ruling elite of Cuscatlán.

Many of the Indians retreated to the mountains, from which they sent out attacks against the Spanish. Alvarado was severely wounded in one battle and ordered his force back to Guatemala. Alvarado returned to El Salvador in 1525. After a long, bloody struggle, he established control over the area and founded the city of San Salvador near Cuscatlán. By 1540, Spanish domination of El Salvador was complete. It was made a province of New Spain (Mexico) and placed under the control of the Captaincy General of Guatemala, where it remained until independence in 1821.

COLONIAL LIFE

The Spanish found El Salvador well populated with Indian groups of diverse cultural backgrounds. In addition to the Pipil and the Lenca, they found Pokoman Indians, related to the Maya, in the northwest, and Matagalpa Indians, of South American origin, in Lenca territory. It has been estimated that from 116,000 to 130,000 Indians lived in El Salvador at the time of the conquest. Some have estimated the population was as high as 500,000. By 1551, war and European diseases had reduced the Indian population to between 50,000 and 60,000. Ill treatment also contributed to the sharp drop in their numbers.

On the heels of the conquistadores came the religious orders. They established churches and monasteries to convert the Indians, teaching them Christian ideals and the Spanish language. Many converted to Catholicism because the alternative was death.

Spanish economic demands and Christianizing activities dictated every aspect of the Indians' lives. They were divided into villages, preventing them from maintaining their former ties with large groups. The Indians were forced to give up much of their

*Above: The Spaniards topple
a religious altar used by
the Salvadoreans.
Right: If the Indians
did not attend church,
they were severely punished.*

culture. All symbols of their religion were destroyed, as well as the picture books that had recorded their history.

The new colony had little mineral wealth, so it attracted fewer settlers than did other colonies in the New World. The conquistadores were interested in military exploits and wealth, not in governing and agriculture.

In order to reward the conquistadores and encourage them to stay, the Spanish Crown introduced the *encomienda* system to replace slavery. An encomienda was a grant given by the Spanish Crown, allowing a Spanish landholder to collect tribute (taxes) from the Indians. Although it began as a means of obtaining taxes, it eventually was used to enslave the Indians and seize their lands.

As it had been for the Indians, farming continued to be the primary economic activity of the Spanish, along with cattle ranching. In the late 1500s, cacao came to be an important export crop. The Indians had long grown cacao, using it as currency and to make chocolate.

*Because there was such a demand for indigo in Europe,
the Indians were forced to work on the indigo plantations.*

Indigo also was grown by the Indians during pre-conquest
times. The leaves of the shrub were used for blue dye. In the 1700s
European demand for indigo soared, due to increased textile
production, and it became a major Salvadorean export. The indigo
boom was a major force in changing El Salvador from a largely
Indian country in 1600 to one where Spanish culture
predominated.

The main source of labor for indigo production was the system
of *repartimiento*, which replaced encomienda. Repartimiento was a
system of forced labor, whereby Spanish authorities could impose
work on the Indians for a fixed number of days at a set wage.
Work on indigo plantations removed Indians from their villages
and contributed to the breakdown of their communities and way
of life.

The growth of *haciendas* (large estates) paralleled the rise of
indigo production and introduced the European feudal concept of
land ownership. Haciendas often developed from a small farm

Hacendados took vast tracts of land, such as these pictured above, from the Indians to grow coffee (left) and sugarcane (right).

located between Indian villages. *Hacendados* (hacienda owners) took Indian land and instituted a system of debt peonage. Under this system, money would be advanced to a worker on a hacienda. A debt was established, which the worker never managed to repay, and which could be inherited.

By the eighteenth century, a small number of hacendados owned much of the productive land and controlled large numbers of Indians. They held great economic, social, and political power, but spent their growing wealth on themselves rather than on the general welfare. Hacendados were either Spanish or Creoles (those of European ancestry born in the New World) and occupied the top level of a rigidly defined Salvadorean society. *Mestizos* (those of mixed Indian and European blood) were at the bottom of the social ladder. By the end of the eighteenth century, they comprised the majority of the population. Indians did not count at all in Salvadorean society.

INDEPENDENCE

Spain's control over its Central American colonies was highly centralized. The colonial system had been structured to benefit Spain rather than the needs of the colonies. During this period, Spain was only one of a number of colonial powers that followed the economic policy of mercantilism. The major trading nations of England, France, Prussia, and Spain held that colonies existed solely for the benefit of the mother country.

Trade was forbidden among the colonies and taxes were high. In El Salvador, the western portion was administered from Guatemala City. The rest was part of the municipality of San Salvador, whose mayor was appointed directly by the crown. The Spanish landowners in El Salvador came to resent Spanish greed, which drained off their riches.

On September 15, 1821, the Captaincy General of Guatemala followed the example of Mexico and declared its independence from Spain. This date is still commemorated as El Salvador's official Independence Day. Spain did not resist, as it was too weak from wars in Europe and America. On July 1, 1823, five Central American colonies—Costa Rica, El Salvador, Guatemala, Honduras, and Nicaragua—formed the United Provinces of Central America. For the next seventeen years, the federation was beset by disagreement over national policies and borders. A major problem was that Central Americans did not see themselves primarily as Central Americans, but as Salvadoreans or Nicaraguans first.

Dissension and revolt among Liberals and Conservatives further divided the federation and kept Central America in chaos for generations. Conservatives opposed any reforms, wanting instead to retain the rigid social structure of the old Spanish rule. Inspired by the same ideals that sparked revolutions in other parts of the world, Liberals called for more extensive social and economic reforms. They gained control of the government and adopted the constitution of 1824, which did away with many of the special privileges and power that Spain had granted to nobles and clergy, and introduced public education.

Despite their differences, neither side questioned the basic social system of private property or agriculture products grown for export. Nor did they attempt to deal with social inequalities and the economic plight of the Indians, who had been excluded from the independence process. This would have threatened the wealth available for the elite.

The Indians resented the way they were being treated and began to rebel. In 1833 Anastasio Aquino led the first major Indian rebellion in the vicinity of Santiago Nonualco, a traditional Pipil area. With an army of four thousand Indian volunteers from surrounding areas, Aquino managed to gain control over a sizable area. His main goal was land for Indians, and he used the slogan embraced nearly a century later by the Mexican revolutionary Emiliano Zapata, "Land for those who work it." Although their numbers were greater, Aquino's army was no match for the better-equipped government army. Aquino escaped and survived in the hills until his capture two months later. He was tried and executed in June 1833.

By 1840, the Conservatives gained control of the federation, but by then it was too late. Unable to survive the constant upheavals, the federation dissolved and the following year El Salvador adopted a constitution as an independent nation.

Chapter 4

THE MODERN REPUBLIC

When El Salvador became an independent nation in 1841, many hoped that peace and stability would finally come, but it was not to be. Conflicts between Liberals and Conservatives continued in the form of civil wars and open strife within and between Central American republics. During this period, the stage was set for more than a century of struggle, marked by dictator following dictator, political turmoil, economic and social injustice, and violence— culminating in a bloody civil war.

THE FIRST SIXTY YEARS

With the demise of the federation in 1840, a new power structure of conservative *caudillos,* or strongmen, arose. They wanted a government similar to the colonial one and supported a stronger church, a society run by elite landholders and merchants, and respect for Spanish heritage.

A small group of wealthy landowners comprised an oligarchy, a government controlled by a few to further and protect their own interests. Many belonged to European families who owned large parcels of land and had become wealthy during the colonial period. The country's wealth came under the ownership of this oligarchy, known as the Catorce Grande—Big Fourteen or Fourteen Families. (Today the Catorce Grande includes about two hundred families with interests in agriculture, industry, and banking.) The oligarchy ran the government and conducted the nation's affairs to promote its own interests.

LAND AND COFFEE

By the mid-1800s, the economy was still largely based on subsistence agriculture, indigo, and cattle. The new economic freedom resulting from independence, however, prompted those in power to begin planting coffee as an export corp. Coffee was a popular drink in Europe, and the demand for the aromatic beans was great. By 1880 coffee overtook indigo as El Salvador's major export crop.

Until now, the ruling elite had consisted primarily of the wealthy hacendados, who lived in the countryside. With the growth of the coffee industry, however, a new coffee oligarchy emerged, gaining control of the government in 1871. These were the city people who had large amounts of money to invest in starting up coffee plantations—doctors, merchants, lawyers, and priests.

This new, liberal elite monopolized power for the next sixty years. Their primary goal was unrestricted economic growth. To achieve this goal, they encouraged coffee production, built railways to ports of foreign trade, eliminated communal lands because they were not used for export crops, and kept the rural population firmly in control.

Coffee production required more land and labor than did indigo. The best land for growing coffee beans was on the upper valley

After being picked, the ripe coffee beans (left) are spread in the drying areas of coffee mills (right).

slopes and the sides of volcanoes. These areas traditionally had been densely populated by Indians, who were able to meet their basic needs from subsistence farming. The new coffee oligarchy had to devise a means whereby they could obtain this land, along with labor for the *fincas* (coffee plantations).

Their solution was the Land Reform Act of 1881. The measure in effect took away the Indians' common lands. It gave the land to large landowners for production of coffee—then cotton and sugarcane—for the world market. The act dramatically changed the Indian and colonial system of land tenure and led to a rapid increase of a landless peasant population.

Between 1860 and 1890, half of the land in El Salvador was turned into private property. A handful of ruling elite controlled most of the best farmland. They passed legislation, including anti-vagrancy laws, to guarantee a labor supply for the coffee plantations. Rural police were created to force peasants to work on the fincas and punish them if they left before the work was done. The wages were barely enough to feed their families.

Material economic growth was the prime goal of the ruling elite. They believed dictators and the military were necessary to keep the booming export trade under control. El Salvador's first dictator was Santiago Gonzáles. He assumed the presidency in 1871 and two years later made himself dictator. Since then, El Salvador has had a history of military governments.

In 1886, a new constitution was written that provided for an effective democratic process. In reality, however, the power remained in the hands of individuals, rather than in causes or movements. All leaders were chosen and backed by their predecessors, usually with the support of the oligarchy.

All of these measures worked and commerce boomed. The immense profits made were not put back into the country, however, but into imported manufactured goods and foreign banks. Modernization of transportation and communication that came with coffee could have led to development of the country's resources. It instead created a rich and powerful elite.

The ruling elite's obsession for power and wealth in the nineteenth century resulted in a number of long-range patterns that persist today. These include reliance on export agriculture, unequal land distribution, social and economic injustice, repression, and postponement of democracy.

THE TWENTIETH CENTURY

The first few decades of the twentieth century were marked by a booming coffee industry, more concentration of land in the hands

After the Panama Canal was built, trade and investments grew in El Salvador and other Central American countries.

of a few, and increasing landlessness and poverty among the peasants. Tension and repression also grew in the countryside. Some of the peasants wanted to form unions to better their situation. The government responded in 1907 by banning trade union organizing among agricultural workers. In 1912, the National Guard was formed. Its main function was to control the rural population and protect coffee plantations.

During the 1800s, Great Britain had been El Salvador's major trading partner. The United States showed little interest in the tiny republic until the early 1900s. Because United States investments were small compared with those in other Central American republics, El Salvador was able to have more independent policies. The construction of the Panama Canal, along with growing United States investments, increased Central America's importance. The United States became more politically involved in the region, wanting to ensure peace to protect its interests. With trade and investments in El Salvador growing rapidly, the United States replaced Great Britain as the major foreign power in El Salvador.

Although the economy was booming, conditions for farm workers as well as city workers were poor. Workdays were as long as fifteen hours, but pay was so low that workers could barely provide enough food for their families. The growth of export agriculture took over land that had provided a living for small farmers and was the source of much of the country's food. As food production declined, basic grains such as corn had to be imported. Rapid population growth increased the number of peasants forced to rely on landowners for work or for a subsistence plot in exchange for work. Finding little work in the country, large numbers of peasants began moving to towns and cities to look for jobs, which were few.

In the 1920s, workers began organizing for change. Many had been influenced by the ideals of the Mexican and Russian revolutions. They wanted shorter working hours, the right to unionize and to strike, a minimum wage, free education for all, and social equality. Fearful of losing its control over workers, the government suspended many civil liberties and used the army against opposition.

The stock market crash in 1929, and the world economic crisis that followed, sent coffee prices tumbling. By this time, coffee had comprised 95 percent of all exports, so the effects on the Salvadorean economy were shattering. Unemployment skyrocketed and wages were cut by the coffee elite, who did little to ease the social tension caused by the Depression.

Discontent among workers set the stage that year for El Salvador's first free election. Alberto Araujo, a reform candidate who had promised widespread changes, was elected by a huge

President Hernández Martínez cutting the ribbon to open the Cuscatlán Bridge across the Lempa River, which was an important new link in the Pan-American Highway

margin. After less than a year in office, he was overthrown by the military and replaced by General Maximiliano Hernández Martínez.

HERNÁNDEZ MARTÍNEZ AND LA MATANZA

In 1932, peasants and workers planned an uprising in the western part of the country. They were led by Augustín Farabundo Martí, the son of a wealthy landowner. Farabundo Martí had helped to found the Central American Socialist party, a group that worked to obtain basic rights for workers. As Izalco Volcano erupted on the night of January 22, 1932, and a fine ash hung in the air, hundreds of peasants, most of them Indian, descended on the towns with machetes.

The military quickly put down the insurrection and, in revenge, systematically massacred an estimated thirty thousand peasants. Anyone with Indian features and wearing peasant clothes was rounded up, even if he or she had not participated in the

Today's guerrillas call their organization the Farabundo Martí National Liberation Front (FMLN). A truckload of FMLN members on patrol (above) and two of the many women who belong to FMLN (left)

rebellion. In the town of Izalco, a group of fifty men were shot. Other victims were forced to dig mass graves for themselves just before being machine-gunned. The mass slaughter came to be known as *La Matanza* (The Massacre). Farabundo Martí was tried and convicted. He died before a firing squad and his name was erased from history. Today, El Salvador's guerrilla army bears the name of Farabundo Martí, who is their hero.

With La Matanza, the military crushed the rising worker and peasant movements and assumed a fierce grip on the country that it has never released.

General Hernández Martínez ruled for twelve years, longer than any other Salvadorean president. He has been called the most notorious modern dictator, creating a military regime that lasted more than fifty years. Hernández Martínez took strong measures to protect the economic interests of the landowning and business elite and stabilize the economy. He passed legislation to discourage further industrialization and turned the economy back over to the coffee growers.

In the 1960s, the economy could no longer depend solely on coffee,
so other crops such as cotton (left) were planted.
Right: Signs of some of the foreign investors operating in El Salvador

DEVELOPMENT AND MODERNIZATION

For the next five decades, the military enjoyed the power of
government and the oligarchs enjoyed the fruits of the economy.
After World War II, El Salvador experienced an economic boom
that lasted through the 1960s. The military's strong grip provided
a stable investment climate that, along with tax incentives and
plentiful cheap labor, attracted foreign investors. During this
period, more than fifty large corporations began operating in El
Salvador. Most were United States based, with names like
Westinghouse, Procter & Gamble, and ESSO.

El Salvador underwent a period of modernization. Low-cost
housing and schools were built, and transportation and electrical
generation facilities for growing industrialization were developed.
Realizing the economy could no longer depend upon coffee alone,
the government shifted emphasis to new crops, such as cotton,
and expanded industry. This growth resulted in the rise of a small
middle class.

Much of the economic growth was impelled by the Alliance for Progress and the Central American Common Market. The Alliance for Progress was a United States-Latin American program that went into effect in 1961. The alliance was partly a response to the Cuban Revolution of 1959, which threatened United States dominance in the region. It pushed for certain reforms in Central America to control the spread of communism. The alliance increased United States influence and investment in El Salvador. The Central American Common Market also was established in 1961. It allowed for unrestricted trade among five of the Central American republics—Honduras, El Salvador, Guatemala, Costa Rica, and Nicaragua.

POVERTY GROWS

Despite the economic boom, most Salvadoreans failed to benefit. Conditions in the countryside had only grown worse for the peasants. The expansion of new crops pushed even more peasants off the land to make way for cotton and sugarcane. Between 1961 and 1975, the number of landless peasants increased from 11 percent to 40 percent of the rural population. Mechanization on farms and fincas reduced the need for workers.

The growth of manufacturing in the cities created few new jobs for the thousands who poured in from the countryside looking for work. This was due to labor-saving technology introduced by United States firms. The unemployed were forced to live in slums, called *tugurios*, with no electricity, running water, or sanitation.

Many peasants moved to neighboring Honduras to escape conditions of landlessness, unemployment, poverty, and the increased population density. By 1965, as many as 350,000

*Damage done in Honduras (above)
by the Salvadorean army
during the "Soccer War."
Workers, in 1979, demonstrating for
higher wages (left) after they
had taken over a cotton mill.*

Salvadoreans were living in Honduras. But tensions between the two countries were high, primarily over their disputed common border and the growing pressure placed on the Honduran economy by Salvadorean immigrants.

In 1969, Honduras began deporting tens of thousands of Salvadoreans. On July 14, war broke out between the two countries. It was called the "Soccer War" because it began shortly after the World Cup playoff matches between both countries. Although the conflict lasted less than a week, it killed three thousand.

The sudden influx of 130,000 Salvadorean refugees increased pressure on the land and calls for land reform. Attempts at land reform over the years had always been met with resistance by the ruling elite, which remained the dominant power. Instead of reforms, the government began to torture opposition leaders.

By the early 1970s, conditions of landlessness, unemployment, poverty, and overpopulation led many to form mass opposition groups, called "popular organizations." For the first time since La

Marchers burned flags to protest the military-backed government.

Matanza, peasant groups were becoming a major factor. Joined by students, professionals, workers, women, and church members, they pressed for social justice. Many participated in civil disobedience—nonviolent resistance to the government or laws believed to be unjust or discriminatory. Their methods included strikes, street demonstrations, and occupations of public buildings, factories, and large estates.

Fearing the growing power of the opposition, the government, oligarchy, and military stepped up violence and repression. Backing up the army were the government security forces and death squads, comprised of several groups that participated in kidnapping, torture, and murder. The National Guard operated primarily in rural areas.

In urban areas, the National Police performed many of the same functions as the National Guard. The Treasury Police was legally required only to enforce customs regulations. In reality, it operated similarly to the National Guard and National Police.

Heavily armed soldiers (left) patrol the streets.
A grandmother (above) holds a sign denouncing
the disappearance of her grandson.

The precursor of the Salvadorean death squads was a right-wing paramilitary group called the Democratic Nationalist Organization (ORDEN). It was formed in 1968 by a Salvadorean general, a highly paid consultant to the CIA (Central Intelligence Agency), who described it as "the body and bones of the army in the countryside." Armed volunteer members acted as the eyes and ears of the armed forces, collaborating with the latter to terrorize and eliminate dissenters. Its fifty thousand plus members were rewarded with access to credit and jobs.

The *escuadrones de muerte* (death squads) began making their deadly rounds in the mid-1970s. Six major death squads participated in a systematic and widespread program of torture, "disappearances," and individual and mass killings of men, women, and children. United States officials and international human rights groups linked death squads with the Salvadorean government.

LIBERATION THEOLOGY

During the 1960s, an important religious movement arose throughout most of Latin America, including El Salvador. Liberation theology taught that poor peasants were equal in God's eyes to the wealthy hacendados. Rather than being the result of divine will, poverty resulted from the wealthy's greed.

Religious leaders, who had begun to interpret the Gospel in the light of social conditions, told peasants and workers that they had the right to seek justice here and now on earth.

One of the first priests to practice liberation theology in El Salvador was Father Rutilio Grande, a Salvadorean-born Jesuit. Along with other religious and lay workers, Father Grande helped establish Bible study and discussion groups called Christian base communities in hundreds of villages. During meetings, members read a passage of scripture and discussed it in terms of their daily lives. They were then encouraged to implement their ideas in some form of social action.

By promoting community organization, the base communities became the seed of a genuinely independent peasant movement. Peasants began organizing agricultural cooperatives, rural unions, and organizations like the Christian Peasants Federation. They demanded access to land, affordable prices for seeds, fertilizer, and credit, and more tolerable working conditions on the haciendas.

The base communities, along with the nuns and priests who supported liberation theology, came to be known as the "popular church." The government called them threatening and subversive. Wealthy landowners called the Jesuits "Communists" and the base communities "cells" (the primary unit of a Communist organization).

José Napoleón Duarte photographed in 1972

ON THE BRINK OF CIVIL WAR

The presidential election of 1972 was a turning point in the growing conflict. Many people still believed that reform was possible without revolution. One of them was José Napoleón Duarte, the mayor of San Salvador and the favored presidential candidate. He belonged to the progressive Christian Democratic party, which was formed to improve conditions for workers and poor people. Duarte won the election, but the military canceled the results and installed the official party's candidate. Duarte was arrested, tortured, and exiled to Venezuela.

The overtly fraudulent election laid the basis for the armed conflict of the 1980s. Peasants and workers had put their faith in politics and elections as a peaceful means of reform. They proved to be ineffectual and their hopes were crushed. Another dishonest election in 1977 led many Salvadoreans to escalate their opposition. By March 1979, strikes were paralyzing the economy and social unrest was widespread. Civil war was coming.

The government's reaction was even greater and more brutal repression, especially in the countryside. Opposition leaders were kidnapped and tortured. There were political arrests, killings, and

The funeral procession of Father Rutilio Grande in San Salvador in 1977

disappearances. Most of the victims were peasants, but they also included union leaders, teachers, students, professionals, and anyone else trying to change the system. In order to defend themselves, peasants formed guerrilla groups to provide protection from the army and an end to military rule.

Violence and repression were stepped up against members of the popular church. A death squad called the White Warriors Union circulated flyers that said, "Be a patriot, kill a priest." On March 12, 1977, Father Rutilio Grande was shot to death.

A month before Grande's assassination, Oscar Arnulfo Romero had become the new archbishop of El Salvador. The shy, scholarly archbishop was a conservative member of the hierarchy of the Catholic church, which was an ally of the military and oligarchy. Archbishop Romero had been a good friend of Father Grande, and his murder created a period of personal crisis and conversion.

Archbishop Romero began to speak out against the repression and injustice. He became one of the most famous and loved church leaders in El Salvador. His work on behalf of the poor earned him a nomination for the Nobel Peace prize. Archbishop Romero's weekly sermons brought hope and information on national events to thousands of people. They were broadcast over the Catholic radio station and became the country's most popular program. He used to say, "The Church is not against the government. The truth is that the government is against the people and we are with the people."

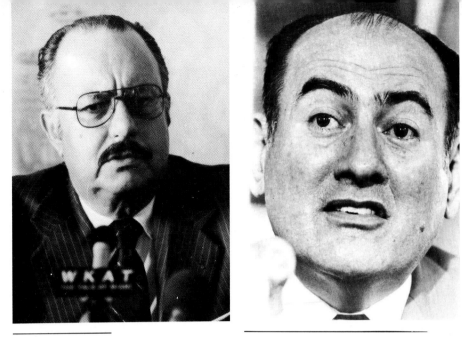

Anastasio Somoza   *General Carlos Humberto Romero*

Events during 1979 in neighboring Nicaragua further alarmed the Salvadorean government and encouraged the popular movement. Since 1937, Nicaragua had been ruled by members of the Somoza family. Their regime has been described as the longest, most corrupt dictatorship in Latin America. In July 1979, a revolution led by the broad-based Sandinista National Liberation Front overthrew dictator Anastasio Somoza.

In a desperate attempt to avoid the brewing civil war in their own country, a group of young, reform-minded Salvadorean military officers overthrew the government of General Carlos Humberto Romero in October 1979. They installed a *junta* (council) made up of two military and three civilian leaders. Many hoped this would be El Salvador's revolution, ending the oligarchy and repression. The junta promised extensive land reform and an end to repression. It was powerless, however, between the civilian reformers and the military. The civilians in the government resigned because they could not make the changes they believed were needed. This left control of the government to the military, which continued the repression.

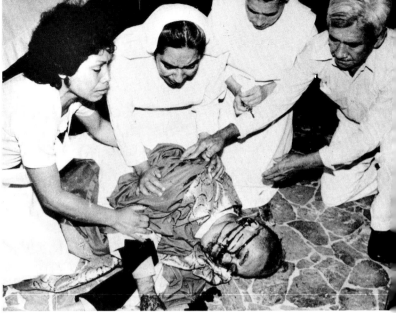

Shortly after giving a sermon in the chapel of a hospital (left), Archbishop Oscar Romero was assassinated (right).

In a speech broadcast to the nation, Roman Catholic Archbishop Oscar Romero asked United States President Jimmy Carter not to give the junta additional military aid.

"The junta and the Christian Democrats do not govern the country. Political power is in the hands of unscrupulous military men who only repress the people and favor the interests of the Salvadorean oligarchy."

On March 23, 1980, Oscar Romero delivered what would be his last sermon. Appealing directly to the Salvadorean people, he said, "No soldier is obliged to obey an order against the will of God. . . . In the name of God and the name of this suffering people, I ask you, I beg you, I order you in the name of God, stop the repression."

While celebrating a memorial mass the following day, he was shot dead by an assassin. To this day, no one has been convicted for killing Archbishop Romero. Opposition leaders subsequently joined forces and called for armed insurrection. El Salvador was plunged into a violent and bloody civil war.

Chapter 5

A TROUBLED NATION

Since 1980, El Salvador has been racked by civil war. On one side are the oligarchy, the military, and the government who fiercely want to defend the status quo and often equate reform with communism. On the other side are poor people, students, workers, peasants, professionals, and religious workers who want social, economic, and political reforms. They have formed their own army to fight the government army. Both sides believe they are in the right.

People are fighting the government over three basic issues. The first, and most important, is the deep economic inequity suffered by the majority of the population. Second is the inability of the political system to allow for change through nonviolent, democratic means. And third is the harsh repression of human rights that has followed attempts at peaceful change.

FROM JUNTAS TO ELECTIONS

The October 1979 junta attempted to address the nation's serious problems. Its failure led to the formation of a second council in 1980 with several Christian Democrats. It, too, collapsed after several months, in part because of the death-squad murder of Christian Democratic Attorney General Mario Zamora. Army officers then asked José Napoleón Duarte, who had returned from exile, to join a third council. He was named president of the council in December 1980 and remained in that capacity until 1982.

Duarte spoke of land reform, democracy, and the need to end the violence. The new government began a land reform program. It took over many of the country's large farms and began distributing them to poor farmers. The government also seized control of the banks and foreign trade.

Despite the fact that El Salvador had its first civilian president in more than fifty years, the military still controlled the real power. With the support of the wealthy landowners, it organized the most sweeping campaign of repression since La Matanza of 1932. The army's aim was to stop the reforms, to eliminate the mass opposition organizations, and to create an environment of terror so strong that no new opposition movements could grow.

It soon became apparent that Duarte and the Christian Democrats could not stop the violence. Between 1980 and 1981, more than twenty-one thousand civilians were killed. Human rights groups, such as Amnesty International and the Americas Watch Committee, have attributed four out of five of these killings to government forces, ORDEN (in its new form of the Nationalist Democratic Front), and right-wing death squads.

Security forces, often operating as death squads at night, targeted anyone merely suspected of leftist sympathies. Mutilated bodies were found daily in ditches, streets, and lakes. The coal-black lava fields of El Playón became an infamous dumping ground for bodies.

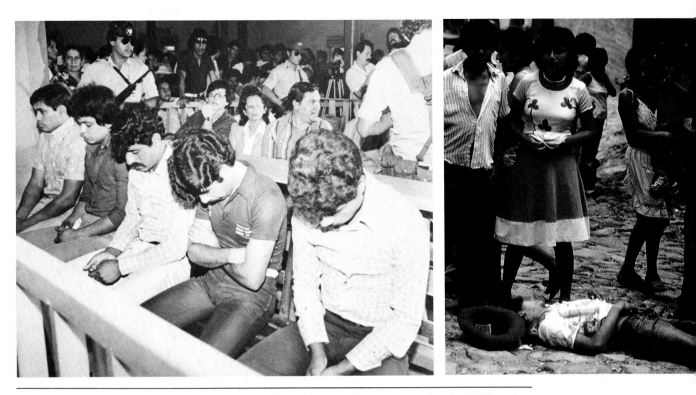

Left: The trial of the national guardsmen who were convicted of killing four
United States churchwomen. Right: Witnesses said Treasury
Police were responsible for the killing of this 17-year-old boy.

On December 2, 1980, security forces abducted, raped, and
killed four United States churchwomen, three of them nuns, who
were doing relief work among refugees in El Salvador. Four years
later, following pressure from the United States, which had briefly
suspended economic aid, six national guardsmen were convicted
of the killings.

A NEW CONSTITUTION

In 1982, the government called for the election of a temporary
legislature that would create a new constitution and organize
presidential elections. The election was largely inspired by the
United States to improve the Salvadorean government's tarnished
image.

The election put the most conservative political and military individuals firmly in power and signaled an end to reform efforts. They were led by Roberto D'Aubuisson, a former military intelligence officer, who earlier had been removed from the army because of his reputation for brutality. Former United States Ambassador Robert White once referred to him as a "pathological killer." D'Aubuisson has been implicated in the murders of Archbishop Oscar Romero and Christian Democrat Mario Zamora.

D'Aubuisson led a newly created party that was extremely right wing and violently anti-Communist. The Nationalist Republican Alliance (ARENA) promised to abolish the United States-supported land reform and to use the security forces to crush all opposition.

The new constitution, adopted December 6, 1983, declares El Salvador to be a democratic republic. In reality, the military and wealthy landowners continue to hold most of the political power. The constitution provides for a president and vice-president, who head the government. Both are elected by direct popular vote for five-year terms. A sixty-member National Assembly, which makes the country's laws, is elected for a three-year term. The president appoints a cabinet to carry out the government's operations.

The judicial system is headed by a Supreme Court, whose thirteen members are elected by the National Assembly. El Salvador is divided into fourteen departments. Each department is headed by a governor appointed by the president. The departments are subdivided into *municipios* (townships) governed by a council elected by the people for a three-year term.

Although moderate José Napoleón Duarte was elected president in 1984, he and the Christian Democratic party began to lose

Left: José Napoleón Duarte is sworn in as president in 1984.
Right: In 1988 Alfredo Cristiani (center) celebrates his
victory with his wife and running mate Francisco Merino.

popularity due to their failure to provide meaningful reforms,
control the military, and end the war. Following municipal and
legislative elections in 1988, Roberto D'Aubuisson's National
Republican Alliance defeated the Christian Democrats, marking
another major swing to the far right.

In May 1988, President Duarte was diagnosed as having cancer.
American military surgeons, who operated on Duarte in the
United States, said a tumor on his liver could not be removed and
would eventually be fatal. Duarte's illness only added to the
problems of the Christian Democratic party, which faced strong
opposition in the 1989 presidential elections.

In March 1989, wealthy businessman Alfredo Cristiani, the
National Republican Alliance's candidate, won a majority in the
presidential elections. Cristiani was inaugurated president on
June 1. Many wondered whether Cristiani or Roberto
D'Aubuisson would hold power.

ELECTIONS AND WAR

Since 1982, elections have occurred in the midst of a violent civil war that has racked a country having no tradition of democratic elections. Many Salvadoreans believe it is impossible to have fair elections under these circumstances. They say that the conditions for a legitimate election do not exist, pointing out a lack of freedom of speech, press, and assembly. A 1983 United Nations report said that in El Salvador there was "a consistent pattern of violations of civil and political rights of all kinds."

One reason opposition candidates have not participated in elections is a fear of violence from the right. In 1980, for example, government security forces tortured and murdered five top opposition leaders after kidnapping them from a meeting. In 1983, the body of the highest ranking opposition leader remaining in El Salvador was found along with three other bodies. A death squad claimed responsibility for his death.

Critics say that many people turn out to vote for fear of not voting. At the polls, voters receive a stamp on their national identity cards. Salvadoreans are required to carry this card, called a *cedula*, at all times. Anyone without this stamp is considered a guerrilla sympathizer and that label can warrant a death sentence. Furthermore, ballot boxes are transparent and ballots are numbered. The number is recorded on a list beside the voter's name.

The United States maintains that since 1982 El Salvador has witnessed free and honest elections in its quest to build democratic institutions. It points to high voter turnout as an indication of the Salvadorean people's commitment to democracy,

Hundreds of people waited in line to vote in 1982.

describing the opposition as a Communist insurrection. The establishment of democracy and the consequent improvement in the human rights situation are cited as the most important changes in El Salvador since the early 1980s.

American observers at the election in March 1989 say it was a free and honest election.

Critics counter that without a democratic tradition, but burdened by a violent history of corrupt elections and military death squads, El Salvador cannot be expected to move overnight from feudalism to a workable democratic system.

THE OPPOSITION

The assassination in March 1980 of Archbishop Oscar Romero was the catalyst for the creation of the popular opposition coalition called the Democratic Revolutionary Front (FDR). The FDR is a coalition of left and center opposition parties and the popular mass organizations of peasants, trade unions, and professional groups. It includes virtually all of El Salvador's opposition groups and forms the political arm of the opposition. The FDR carries out active political education and organization, as well as providing the diplomatic presence of the Salvadorean opposition to the outside world. The FDR has its headquarters in San Salvador.

The Democratic Revolutionary Front presented a platform that promised to replace the current economic system with a "new society." Banking, foreign trade, electricity generation, petroleum refining, and "monopolistic enterprises in industry, trade, and services" would be nationalized. It also promised land reform, economic planning, strict respect for human rights, and popular participation in the management of government.

The FDR is allied with the Farabundo Martí Front for National Liberation (FMLN), which was formed in October 1980. The FMLN is a coalition of several guerrilla armies and forms the military arm of the opposition. It developed out of Marxist groups and guerrilla organizations. Its members include peasants, priests, teachers, doctors, former government officials, and army deserters.

Many women have joined their ranks. The most well known was Dr. Malida Anaya Montes, a former university professor and founder of ANDES (National Association of Salvadorean Educators), a militant teachers' union. Known as Comandante Ana María, she was a top guerrilla leader until her death in 1983. Comandante Ana Guadelupe Martínez is currently one of the top women leaders of the guerrilla army.

The FMLN began operations in the northern mountainous region with broad support from the rural population, many of whom had relatives killed by the military. They refer to the guerrillas as *los muchachos* (the young ones). By 1985, the FMLN

In 1987 representatives of the FDR and FMLN met for scheduled peace talks with Duarte's government.

functioned as a standing army of an estimated eight thousand regular troops able to coordinate military actions throughout most of the country. By contrast, the Salvadorean army has fifty-five thousand men, with another twenty thousand security forces under army control.

The FDR and FMLN differ in origins and ideology. But they are united in their determination to remove the rule of the oligarchy and the military and replace the old system with massive land reforms and nationalization programs. From its inception, the FDR/FMLN has called for a negotiated settlement of the war. It realizes that a complete military victory would be nearly impossible, given the balance of forces in El Salvador and its strategic location.

CENTRAL AMERICAN PEACE ACCORD

In August 1987, five Central American nations—El Salvador, Costa Rica, Guatemala, Honduras, and Nicaragua—signed the

Central American Peace Accord. The plan was aimed at ending the region's guerrilla wars and ensuring full democratic rights. Its major points were cease-fires and peace talks between governments and rebels; democratic reforms including freedom of the press, speech, and assembly; free elections; economic development; and pardons for political prisoners.

The plan's originator, Costa Rican President Oscar Arias, received the 1987 Nobel Peace prize for his efforts to bring peace to Central America. However, it appeared as though the peace plan would not be carried out because the Central American governments and the opposition groups do not want to give up their power.

In San Salvador fighting between government troops and guerrillas has continued and in 1989 some officials connected with the ARENA party were assassinated.

UNITED STATES INVOLVEMENT

Since the start of civil war, the United States has provided more than $3 billion in military and economic aid to El Salvador. A congressional study reported that three-fourths of this aid has been war related. By 1982, El Salvador had become the world's fourth-largest recipient of United States aid.

The United States has treated Central America as its "backyard" since the Monroe Doctrine of 1823, which asserted America's right to keep hostile, foreign powers out of the Western Hemisphere. By World War II, United States predominance was firmly established.

After World War II, United States policy focused on the East-West struggle, fearing Communist intervention. Since the Cuban revolution in 1959, Washington has been determined to prevent

The United States sent men to train the Salvadorean military.

similar revolutions in the region. In order to protect what it describes as strategic and economic interests, the United States has maintained its dominance in Central America by supporting and collaborating with local landowning, military, and business oligarchies. It also has engaged in repeated direct and indirect military intervention, including a massive militarization of the region.

This military buildup is based on two principles of United States foreign policy: the "domino theory" and the alleged Soviet-Cuban threat in the Caribbean Basin. In essence, the domino theory states that if one nation in the region falls to communism, the rest will follow, presenting a formidable threat to the United States.

The United States has modernized and transformed the Salvadorean military into one of the best equipped and trained counterinsurgency forces in the region. It has provided weapons, aircraft, ammunition, personnel supplies, transport vehicles, and

Guerrillas fighting with captured American weapons

communications gear. United States training has reformed fighting techniques from those of a conventional military to those required for a guerrilla war.

Nonetheless, the army is plagued by low morale. In El Salvador, as in the rest of Central America, only the poor are recruited into the military. For many, it is the only job they can find. Many are simply picked up on street corners or in the countryside and forced to prove themselves in order to survive. To show their toughness, they often have to commit rape and torture as initiation.

With the exception of military leadership, the ranks of the army are filled with peasants and poor urban workers—the same people who are fighting the government. The government soldiers would often rather run than fight, unlike the guerrillas who are powerfully motivated. Many, in fact, have deserted the army to join the FMLN.

During his administration in the late 1970s, United States President Carter had emphasized reform in El Salvador. Ronald Reagan, who was president from 1981-89, changed the issue from one of social justice to an East-West confrontation, emphasizing a military solution. George Bush, who became the United States president in 1989, has maintained this policy in El Salvador.

Economics continues to play a major role in United States policy in Central America. The region's economy is still primarily agricultural and the United States remains its major trading partner and the source of most of its financing. Businesses owned by American corporations stand among the largest enterprises in each country. The United States also emphasizes the strategic importance of protecting shipping lanes and the Panama Canal, as well as access to Mexican and Guatemalan oil fields. Thus, the United States believes it must protect its economic interests— investment, trade, aid, and finance—that dominate the small economies of Central America. It fears any revolutionary government that could threaten those interests.

Critics say the United States refuses to recognize the internal roots of the current unrest in Central America. They argue that it is United States aid that has been instrumental in the continuation of the war. It also has helped to maintain the economic, social, and political injustices that are at the root of the conflict.

The United States refutes the critics and maintains that the Soviets, the Cubans, and now the Nicaraguans direct all political turmoil in the region. El Salvador has become the "test case" of the administration's determination to halt communism in its backyard. Thus, the United States military commitment in Central America has been increased by staggering amounts. Many fear that by insisting on a military solution to a crisis caused by festering injustices, the United States is heading toward direct intervention by its armed forces, which could lead to another Vietnamlike war.

Chapter 6

THE ECONOMY

The Salvadorean economy has been in a serious downward spiral since the outbreak of the civil war in 1980. More than two-thirds of the work force is unemployed or underemployed, wages have fallen by 60 percent, inflation is high, and the cost of living has risen by more than 50 percent. Three-fourths of the rural population, which includes more than half of El Salvador's people, live in absolute poverty.

The war has caused more than $1 billion in damages to homes, crops, and the infrastructure, which includes transportation, utilities, and public buildings, such as schools. The war costs the government $1 million a day, and most of its economic policy is directed toward sustaining the military. One-fourth of El Salvador's annual budget is spent on defense.

The shaky business climate has led to massive capital flight of more than $1 billion, which is the most severe Salvadorean economic problem. Capital flight occurs when local businesses and giant European and American corporations, called multinationals, take money out of the country. Capital flight has been most damaging to manufacturing and few local and foreign businesses have made new investments.

El Salvador's civil war continues to cause millions of dollars of damage.
Left: A bomb explosion in the office of the president of the Supreme Court not only
destroyed the office but injured the president and his secretary as well.
Right: Guerrillas blew up this bridge and cut the highway connection of
the city of San Miguel to Honduras.

The Salvadorean economy continues to function mainly as a result of receiving massive amounts of United States financial aid. United States aid, which has totaled $3 billion since 1980, provides half of El Salvador's annual budget. Without this aid, along with money sent home by Salvadorean refugees living primarily in the United States, the economy would have broken down completely.

A devastating earthquake on October 10, 1986, only added to El Salvador's economic problems. Centered in San Salvador, it caused more than $1.5 billion in damages and left more than 200,000 homeless. Government resources were subsequently focused on reconstruction, diverting funds from social projects and the war effort. Critics charged that the government handled relief efforts poorly, saying that aid rarely or never reached the people who needed it most.

AGRICULTURE

Despite the serious condition of El Salvador's economy, it continues to function. Agriculture remains the largest sector of the economy. It provides about 24 percent of the gross national product, more than three-fourths of all exports, and employs more than half of Salvadorean workers. El Salvador has an agro-export economy based on a system of huge plantations that produce only a few crops for export. The primary crops are coffee, cotton, and sugarcane. Three-fourths of El Salvador's land is used for cropland and pasture, with more than one-fourth of this for coffee. Because the economy relies so heavily on just a few crops, it is very vulnerable to fluctuations in international demand and prices.

El Salvador still produces more coffee than any other Central American country. Until 1950, coffee provided nearly 90 percent of its export revenues. By 1986, it still produced 72 percent of all export earnings. Most coffee is shipped to West Germany.

INDUSTRY AND TRADE

Until 1979, El Salvador was the region's leading exporter of manufactured goods. Manufacturing continues to be the second-largest contributor to the gross national product. It accounts for about 15 percent of the national income and employs about 22 percent of the work force. Since the start of the war, more than thirty-five multinationals have left the country. By 1985, there were still about 130 United States businesses in El Salvador, including forty-eight multinationals. Three of the top five United States oil companies—Exxon (formerly ESSO), Texaco, and Chevron—are still active in El Salvador.

Left: Young coffee plants ready to be planted in the ground
Right: A coffee taster at work

Most of the large corporations are involved in manufacturing, especially in food processing, tobacco, bottling, and textiles. Principal products are cotton textiles, shoes, cosmetics, furniture, chemicals and fertilizers, petroleum products, and cigarettes.

El Salvador's top trading partners are the United States, West Germany, Japan, and the Central American Common Market. Its chief imports are automobiles, machinery, other manufactured products, chemicals, and petroleum.

UNIONS

Since 1984, when repression eased in the cities, big business and the government have had to deal with increasing demands from labor unions, which have resumed organizing and strikes. Salvadoreans have had a long history of trade union organizing. After La Matanza of 1932, however, the government banned all unions. Sixteen years later, urban workers were allowed to organize, but rural unions continued to be prohibited.

Despite the government's ban, rural workers began organizing in the 1960s. By the 1970s, urban and rural unions became a powerful force for social and political change. The government, which viewed union leaders as Communists, stepped up its repression against trade unions. Between 1979 and 1982, more than eight thousand Salvadorean trade unionists were murdered, abducted, or wounded.

In 1986, the National Salvadorean Workers' Union (UNTS) was formed to challenge the Duarte government. Comprised of numerous groups including peasant and worker organizations, it became the largest and most diverse labor alliance in the history of El Salvador. The UNTS has called for peace talks, economic and social reform, and democratic freedoms.

TRANSPORTATION AND COMMUNICATION

El Salvador has the most highly developed transportation system in Central America. This is largely the result of its agro-export economy, which requires an efficient means of transporting crops for export. All the major agricultural areas are connected by 6,650 miles (10,702 kilometers) of roads, 980 miles (1,577 kilometers) of which are paved. The northern section near the Honduran border lacks good roads. The Inter-American Highway, which runs the length of Central America, traverses El Salvador from east to west. Only the wealthy own cars, so most people walk, take buses, or travel by mule and ox cart.

Improvements in the highway system since 1950 have overshadowed the importance of railways for commercial transport. Two aging rail lines connect Guatemala and coffee-growing regions with San Salvador and the country's two major

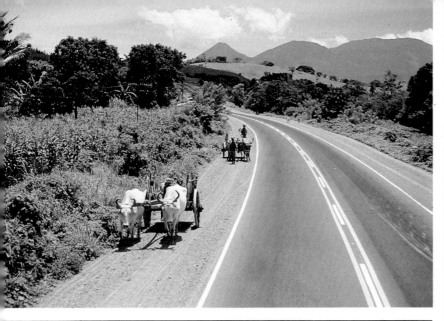

*Primitive ox carts and overcrowded buses are seen
on the highways more often than are cars,
since cars are a luxury only the very wealthy can afford.*

ports. El Salvador's Ilopango International Airport is the largest
and most advanced in Central America. About six airlines provide
international service. Taca is the Salvadorean regional airline,
largely owned by United States investors.

Most Salvadorean news media are reasonably free of censorship
and government control. Most commercial media are, however,
owned by right-wing interests and there is no opposition press.
Two of El Salvador's five television channels feature educational
programs and are government operated. About sixty licensed
radio stations operate in the country. All are commercial except
the government-operated Radio Nacional de El Salvador. The
guerrillas operate two major radio stations. The best known as the
voice of the FMLN is Radio Venceremos, which has been
broadcasting from rebel-controlled Morazán department since
1981.

Five daily newspapers are published in San Salvador. One is
government owned and all range from conservative to
ultraconservative. *La Prensa Gráfica* is the largest newspaper.

Salvadoreans still manage to smile,
despite the struggles of their daily life.

Chapter 7

THE PEOPLE OF
EL SALVADOR

For centuries El Salvador was an Indian land, yet today only small, isolated communities of indigenous people considered to be "Indians" exist in the region. Since the Spanish conquest, El Salvador's once large and varied population of native people has been decimated by massive killings, enslavement and epidemics, intermarriage, and exposure to European culture.

Today less than 10 percent of Salvadoreans are Indian. The vast majority of Salvadoreans are mestizos. About 1 percent are of unmixed white ancestry and belong to the upper class, which is largely comprised of people of Spanish, English, or French descent. Some of them are descended from old families, whose ancestors came to El Salvador within the last several hundred years. Others are immigrants who made their fortunes in coffee, cotton, and politics. All Salvadoreans speak Spanish and most are Roman Catholic.

CLASS DISTINCTION

Family background, wealth, and education determine social and class structure in El Salvador. The three main classes and cultural groups are the upper class, mestizos, and Indians. The term mestizo is not a racial or ethnic term, but is primarily a cultural and class description. The word literally means "mixed." The term *ladino* is sometimes used to refer to mestizos in El Salvador. It has the same meaning, but is used mainly in Guatemala.

Mestizo culture has its origins in both Indian and Spanish culture. Mestizos speak only Spanish, but practice many Indian as well as European customs. The aboriginal corn tortilla and tamale, for example, remain the staff of life, and the Indian planting stick is still used. An Indian who has shed his or her Indian identity may be considered a mestizo.

Salvadorean society assigns different roles to these different groups. The upper class, which is mostly of unmixed European ancestry but includes some mestizos, is the dominant group and enjoys most of the benefits of the society. Mestizos comprise a portion of the small middle class and most of the lower classes. Indians occupy the lowest rung of the social ladder and are largely deprived of any social benefits.

UPPER CLASS

A tiny minority, perhaps 2 percent, belong to El Salvador's upper class, often referred to as the oligarchy, or Catorce Grande. Yet they control the vast majority of the nation's wealth. The elite is comprised of those who have land, those who have investments in industry and commerce, and merchants. All have holdings in

Wealthy Salvadoreans live in luxurious surroundings and have leisure time to enjoy.

each of the important sectors of the economy. In some cases families are related socially through marriage. Others may be related economically through joint investments. Since 1932 there also has been a military element in the elite.

Many of the wealthy elite think of themselves as European in manner and Salvadorean only by birth. They are separated from the masses by social, class, and ethnic differences. They have opulent homes in the city and impressive country estates. They drive Mercedez-Benzes and Volvos to work in modern, air-conditioned offices. Leisure time is plentiful, and much of it is spent at country clubs, which are the center of social life for wealthy Salvadoreans.

MIDDLE CLASS

The emergence of a Salvadorean middle class is relatively recent. It is largely the result of economic growth that began in the

*A middle-class mother and her
son (left) and a mestizo girl (right)*

1950s. Although the middle class is growing, it still comprises
only about 8 percent of the population. The majority are of
unmixed European ancestry, although mestizos also belong to this
class. Most live in San Salvador, although they also live in rural
areas. Many have modern apartments or homes and often own
cars. In the city, the middle class typically work as doctors,
accountants, high-level government officials, lawyers, teachers,
businessmen, and office workers. In the countryside they may be
employed as mechanics, drivers, skilled laborers, and small
farmers.

LOWER CLASS

The vast majority of Salvadoreans belong to the lower class,
which is comprised of mestizos and Indians. About three-fifths
live in the countryside and more than half are unable to find
work. The lower class has suffered the most as a result of the civil

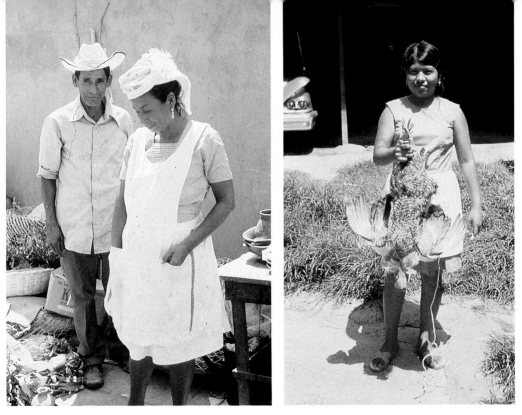

People at the bottom of the social scale find work in street vending (left) or domestic labor, such as this woman (right) who cooks for a middle-class household.

war and the current economic crisis. Half of the labor force receives very meager wages.

People on the upper end of the scale have finished primary school and work as schoolteachers, small landowners, commercial employees, and urban workers. Those at the bottom of the social scale are often called the marginal population. They change jobs frequently and must move to find work. Many are illiterate or have only two or three years of schooling. Typical jobs are wage labor in agriculture, day labor, street vending, and services such as shining shoes and domestic labor.

INDIANS

Salvadoreans use the term *Indio* to refer to the few remaining full-blooded Indians who practice the modern remnants of ancient Indian traditions. The term is also sometimes used disparagingly by the elite. Since 1930, the term *Indian* has not been an official census category, so it is difficult to determine the size and nature of the Indian population. Some sources put the figure at 10 percent of the total population, others at 3 percent. One recent report said there are only thirty-five thousand native Indians in El Salvador, which would be less than 1 percent.

No one disputes the fact that very few Indians remain in El Salvador, and fewer still retain even a modified Indian way of life. Since colonial times, Indians have been encouraged to shed their pre-Columbian culture and assimilate with the dominant society. After La Matanza, when most of those killed were Indians, many purposefully hid their Indian identity.

Most of El Salvador's least acculturated Indians live in the southwest, where pre-Columbian culture was strongest at the time of the conquest. Most are descendants of the Pipil. Enclaves of descendants of other tribes, including the Lenca and Maya, are found in some areas. Matagalpa Indians live in the eastern departments of Morazán and La Unión. Their cultures today are similar to that of the Pipil, due in part to Pipil dominance at the time of the conquest.

Indian culture today is very different from that existing at the time of the Spanish conquest. Only a few remaining culture traits distinguish the Indian from that of lower-class mestizos. These include traditions, customs, costumes, and crafts, as well as remnants of their language and music. By 1975 it was estimated that Indian clothing and festivals were found among 1 percent of the population at most.

Many Pipil Indians live in rural areas, primarily in the southwest, including the townships of Izalco and Nahuizalco in Sonsonate Department. They tend to live as cohesive groups, which may be in the center of town, on the outskirts, or in the

Indian portraits

countryside. In El Salvador, Indians are the poorest of the poor. Very few own land and most work as seasonal agricultural workers, small-scale farmers, artisans, and city laborers. Indian handicrafts are still produced in some towns, but native skills are being lost as handicrafts are replaced by factory wares.

Very few Indians still wear distinctive costumes. Only women in a few villages wear traditional *refajos* (skirts) with plain white or brightly colored blouses. Women in Izalco and Nahuizalco wear them tightly wrapped, while women from Panchimalco wear wide pleated skirts. Ceremonial costumes are sometimes used for special observances.

Although most Indians are Catholic, they have retained some ancient religious beliefs. Some pre-Columbian dances depict the conquest of the Indians in Latin America. Others take place at certain times of the year to win the favor of the gods who control the crops and weather.

A family sharing a meager meal in a refugee camp

FAMILIES

As elsewhere in Latin America, families are the core of Salvadorean culture. Bonds are strong between parents and their children, their grandchildren, and brothers and sisters. Parents work hard to provide a better life for their children. Yet families are very unstable due to widespread poverty and the large number of migrant agricultural workers. They have no job security and must constantly move around looking for work. Men and women must leave their families behind and may not see them for months. Some seldom or never live at home.

Family cohesion has been strained even further by the war in El Salvador. Families have been torn apart by deaths and disappearances, and many have had to flee their homes to escape bullets and bombs. More than one-fifth of Salvadoreans have become homeless as a result of the war; more than a million have left the country.

In rural families, children are viewed, at least in part, as economic resources. If they are able to survive past their fifth year (more than one-third die before this age), it means an extra pair of hands to help with the harvest. In the countryside, one-third of the women become pregnant by the age of fourteen. The average rural woman gives birth eight to ten times, while an urban woman is likely to have at least five children.

About one-fourth of all households are headed by women. In this case a typical home might include a woman, her daughter, her daughter's children, and no husbands. Homes where both parents are present might include their children, a grandparent, and sometimes aunts and uncles. Lower-class women have a double burden. In addition to domestic tasks and child raising, they must earn an income. Many rural women do farmwork. Girls are often pressured to drop out of school early to help care for younger siblings or work in the fields.

The difficulty in finding agricultural work, which is considered to be a man's work, has forced many women to go to the cities, where they work in a wide variety of jobs with low pay. More women than men migrate to urban areas, as it is easier for them to find work as domestics, seamstresses, factory workers, and market vendors.

For centuries, Salvadorean women have had to contend with male attitudes toward women. These are embodied in the word *machismo*, which describes the traditional Latin American view of ideal male qualities. Most Salvadorean men, especially in rural areas, don't believe men and women are equals. They believe men are smarter and more important than women. According to machismo, a woman should be modest, gentle, and uncomplaining.

*Mothers and Relatives of the Assassinated and Disappeared march for
peace, political dialogue, and the release of political prisoners.*

Despite these attitudes, the role of some women is changing in
El Salvador. In the cities, middle-class women believe they should
be able to do whatever they want. In the countryside, the war has
forced women to take on many new responsibilities and learn
new skills.

Throughout El Salvador's turbulent modern history, women
have played an integral role in the struggle for change. Women
market vendors, factory workers, teachers, peasants, and students
have staged protests, strikes, and marches. Many thousands have
been tortured and killed. The Association of Salvadorean Women
(AMES) was founded in 1979. It is a popular organization that
works to mobilize and motivate women to participate in different
aspects of the war effort.

Members of the Committee of Mothers and Relatives of the
Assassinated and Disappeared (COMADRES) have at least one
family member who has been lost because of the war. Wearing
white scarves on their heads, the women hold demonstrations and
marches in San Salvador, demanding that government officials tell
them where their missing relatives are. Increasing numbers of

Left: Holy Week procession   Right: Some of the medicinal herbs used by curanderos

women have joined the guerrillas too. They occupy leadership roles as well as the ranks of combatants.

RELIGION

As in the rest of Latin America, El Salvador is largely a Catholic country. About 80 percent of Salvadoreans are Roman Catholic. The Catholic tradition dates to the Spanish conquest when thousands of Indians were converted to the faith of their conquerors. An estimated 5 percent to 10 percent of Salvadoreans belong to various Protestant denominations, including Lutherans, Baptists, Mennonites, and several Pentecostal groups.

Some Salvadoreans, especially in remote rural areas, often seek the advice of persons called *curanderos*, who are believed to have mystical powers. Curanderos practice the Indian tradition of *brujería*, which is witchcraft, or magic. If the person has problems with illness or with love, the curandero will prescribe rituals and folk remedies (*remedios*) that include special herbs and teas. *Botanicas* are stores that sell herbs used by curanderos.

Right: The wealthy use bars on their windows and stone walls for protection. Below: Most of the people who move to the cities come to San Salvador, which is El Salvador's largest city.

Chapter 8

WAY OF LIFE

San Salvador

Not one aspect of daily life in El Salvador remains untouched by the crippled economy and the civil war. The wealthy have become prisoners in their own homes, barricaded behind huge stone and cement walls topped with coils of barbed wire and shards of broken glass. The poor are prisoners of another sort. Hundreds of years of oppression and exploitation have sentenced the peasants to lives of hunger and poverty, where daily survival is the primary preoccupation.

LIFE IN THE CITIES

Until the 1950s, El Salvador was a predominantly rural country. With the development of industry and trade, towns and cities grew. More and more people began moving to cities looking for work. Today about 40 percent of the nation's population lives in urban areas, which continue to grow steadily.

More than nine-tenths of the people moving to cities come to San Salvador, El Salvador's bustling capital and its largest city. San Salvador sits at the base of San Salvador Volcano in the Valley of the Hammocks, named for its gentle slopes. The verdant peak provides a dramatic backdrop to this modern city of gleaming office buildings, pastel-colored factories, large shopping malls, and

The Presidential Palace (above)
and the famous statue of
El Salvador del Mundo (left)

busy streets. San Salvador serves as the nation's commercial, industrial, and financial metropolis, as well as its political center.

San Salvador was founded in 1525 some twenty-five miles (forty kilometers) north of its present site. It was located near Cuscatlán, the largest Indian city in El Salvador at the time of the conquest. The Spanish named it San Salvador, which means "Holy Savior" in Spanish. A famous statue of El Salvador del Mundo today overlooks downtown San Salvador. It portrays Christ with his arms spread, standing atop a globe of the world.

The city has been completely or partially destroyed by earthquakes and rebuilt numerous times since it was moved to its present location in 1528.

San Salvador is laid out in the shape of a cross, a plan favored by the early Spaniards. The four main, tree-lined avenues meet in the center of the city at the Plaza Barrios, which hums with activity. Most of the city's important buildings are located here,

Views of San Salvador, clockwise from bottom left: A street market, the Metropolitan Cathedral, and the National Palace

including the National Palace, the Metropolitan Cathedral, and the National Theater. Throngs of office workers, shoppers, vendors, businesspeople, laborers, and shoe shine boys clog the broad avenues and narrow side streets.

Nearby is the Mercado Cuartel (Central Market), which covers an entire block and is dedicated mostly to the sale of handicrafts.

The city of San Salvador lies at the base of San Salvador Volcano. The well-to-do live in elegant suburbs (inset) in the surrounding hills.

In the maze of hundreds of tiny covered stalls, shoppers browse among brightly colored sisal bags, woven hammocks, leather goods, and wood carvings. Locals shop here for fresh vegetables, fruit, meat, poultry, and seafood. A short distance away is the Metrocentro, a modern, split-level shopping center and the largest in Central America.

Most of the wealthy live in elegant suburbs, called *colonias*, located in the surrounding hills. They live in expensive, modern homes with swimming pools and well-tended gardens. The San Benito and Escalón districts are two of the city's most exclusive.

Cardboard shacks in San Salvador (left) where the majority of Salvadoreans live illegally. The casino of Santa Ana (above)

Here the elite gather to socialize in sidewalk cafés and continental restaurants, dance in discotheques, and shop in upscale boutiques.

Just below the hilltops are the *barrancas*, ravines and riverbeds lined with shanties and shacks made of tin, cardboard, and cloth. An estimated 60 percent to 75 percent of San Salvador's population lives in illegally built slums with dirt floors, no electricity, and no running water.

Many poor families rent one-room apartments in crowded, decaying buildings called *mesónes*. This is one of the most typical forms of city housing. There are no individual taps or toilets in the rooms, and some have no windows and only mud floors.

Middle-class Salvadoreans live in row houses or comfortable apartments.

Santa Ana is the coffee capital of El Salvador and its second-largest city. It is located in the western region below the inactive Santa Ana Volcano. Santa Ana began as a pre-Columbian Indian

Left: Daily market in Santa Ana
Right: Cotton stored in a
warehouse in San Miguel

village, named Cihuatehuacán (City of the Priests). The city has
grown as a result of its location in the nation's richest coffee-
growing region. Santa Ana is a modern metropolis of schools,
hospitals, colonial-style homes, public buildings, and theaters. The
largest coffee mill in the world sits on the city's outskirts.

San Miguel is the nation's third-largest city. It sits at the foot of
San Miguel Volcano, which is usually smoking and most recently
erupted in 1986. An important distribution center for cotton, it
serves as the commercial center of the eastern region. A large
army garrison is located here.

RURAL LIFE

Three out of five Salvadoreans live in the *campo* (countryside),
which is primarily the domain of the very poor. Sixty percent of

Some other crops grown in El Salvador are tobacco (left) and cacao (right).

the nation's most productive land is owned by a handful of elite
landowners, most of whom trace their lineage from the colonial
era. They grow coffee, cotton, and sugarcane for export on huge
plantations, which may be as large as 3,000 to 6,000 acres (1,214 to
2,428 hectares). Agriculture workers employed full-time on the
plantations are called *colonos*. They live in small hamlets on the
estates.

The majority of Salvadoreans who live in the campo are small
farmers and agricultural workers. Their chief preoccupation is
related to the daily problems of poverty—finding work and
paying for food. Sixty percent of the rural population is landless
and must try to find work on the large plantations. Two out of
five do not earn enough money to pay for a basic diet of corn and
beans.

About 40 percent of rural Salvadoreans are subsistence farmers,

A subsistence farmer works his land with oxen (left). The Pipil Indian village of Izalco (right)

most of whom rent small plots of land. They coax corn, beans, rice, and sorghum out of the poorest of soils. Ninety-five percent of these holdings are too small to provide a living, so the farmers also must work as agricultural laborers to supplement their incomes. With the beginning of the coffee harvest in December, an estimated 300,000 seasonal workers migrate to the plantations.

Salvadorean towns are built around a central square, called a plaza. The plaza is planted with trees, flowers, and shrubs, and may have a fountain in the center. The plaza is a popular spot for relaxing and socializing.

Outside the villages are clusters of small houses connected by dirt paths. The most common kind of home, called a *choza*, uses wattle construction. It is made of woven branches and covered with mud. Those who can afford it live in whitewashed adobe homes, made of sun-dried mud bricks. Adobe homes are in constant danger of cracking or disintegrating during the rainy season. Both kinds of homes usually have thatch or tile roofs.

Most rural Salvadorean homes are small and crowded, with six

Men making adobe (above),
sun-dried bricks
that are used to build homes;
the adobe homes at left
have tile roofs.

to nine people living in one or two rooms. Curtains may be used instead of walls to separate one room from another. Most do not have kitchens, running water, bathrooms, or electricity. They usually have beaten dirt floors and a few pieces of furniture. At night family members pull out cots, mats, or hammocks on which to sleep. Kerosene lamps and candles provide light.

The poorest of the poor are often unable to afford even a home of mud or adobe. They build shanties on plantations, land used for cattle grazing, or anywhere else that might be located near work. They build shelters from anything they can find, including cardboard boxes, scraps of wood, and tin tied with ropes or held down with rocks.

A Salvadorean mother has much work to do. She rises early and may trudge for an hour or so to the nearest source of water. She then gathers firewood to build a fire on a raised platform oven called an *ornilla*. After making the day's supply of tortillas, she toasts them on a *comal* (clay griddle) over the fire. A typical breakfast consists of a diced hot tortilla in fresh, warm milk or a hot salted tortilla and coffee.

In El Salvador it may truly be said that a woman's work is never done.
Left: Washing clothes in a stream   Right: Making pupusas

Farm workers who live in villages leave for the fields by 5:30 A.M. and children who go to school arrive by 8:00 A.M. If the father is at home and unemployed, he may look for a job working in the fields. In addition to cooking all the meals, the mother raises chickens or pigs, tends the garden, washes clothes on rocks in the river, cleans the house, and cares for children too young or sick to attend school or work in the fields. During the harvest season, the entire family works on the plantations.

A Salvadorean woman may sell homemade goods at one of many stands found in cities and the campo. Such items may include homegrown vegetables, candles wrapped in colorful paper, bright red peppers, or *refrescos*, which are homemade fruit drinks. Many also sell homemade food such as tortillas, tamales, and *pupusas*, a popular snack found only in El Salvador. They are made of corn tortillas filled with cheese, pork, or mashed beans and cooked on a griddle.

In the morning many women go to the nearest village for the daily market, which is often held in the plaza. The markets provide an array of colorful flowers, fruits, and vegetables, along with homemade food.

At midday, people take a break called a *siesta*, which is common throughout Latin America. Shops close for an hour or two and people have lunch and take naps or relax before returning to work. Lunch is the largest meal of the day. It may consist of soup, tortillas, rice, beans, cheese, or rarely, some kind of meat—which is usually scarce. Meals may be supplemented by bread, fruits, vegetables, and fish when available. A light supper at the end of the day usually consists of tortillas and red beans.

THE WAR IN THE COUNTRYSIDE

Most of the war's heavy fighting takes place in the countryside. Few areas have remained untouched. Nearly everyone has had a relative or friend killed, tortured, or kidnapped.

The FMLN, El Salvador's armed opposition, is believed to control about 20 percent to 30 percent of El Salvador, mostly in the region north and east of San Salvador. These areas are called "zones of control." Today, more than 300,000 people live in these areas. The FMLN provides medical clinics, schools that teach reading and writing, and agricultural cooperatives. Cooperatives and privately owned farms produce corn, beans, rice, vegetables, eggs, milk, beef, pork, and fish.

Although survival is a struggle, peasants in the zones of control are creating their own democracy, governing themselves with an egalitarian philosophy. Each village has a "popular committee," similar to a town council. Membership is comprised of representatives of each of the community's organizations. The committee typically includes a mayor, a teacher, a health worker, and representatives of farming cooperatives. Leaders are elected by the villagers.

Since 1982, the Salvadorean government has focused on eliminating these zones of control. Army leaders say they want to eliminate support for the guerrillas. Their strategy has included a "scorched earth" policy. The goal is to drain the "sea" (depopulate the countryside) to catch the "fish" (the armed opposition). As a result, much of the war is directed against civilians in the northern and eastern parts of El Salvador. Continued bombing raids are designed to make certain areas uninhabitable.

With extensive United States training and military equipment, Salvadorean troops first "soften" the area they intend to depopulate by bombing it. After several hours of aerial bombardment, troops on the ground close in on the targeted village. As they move on, they kill all the livestock, burn crops, and destroy any structures their bombs left standing. Remaining civilians are forcibly removed from communities believed to provide support for the FMLN.

International human rights monitoring organizations have pointed out that these actions violate the laws of the Geneva Conventions. These laws prohibit displacement of civilian populations and destruction of crops and foodstuffs, livestock, or anything else necessary for their survival.

REFUGEES

Today there are more political refugees in exile from El Salvador than there are from any other Latin American country except Chile. The military's efforts to "drain the sea" have left more than 600,000 Salvadoreans homeless in their own nation. As many as one million have fled to the United States to seek refuge. Within El

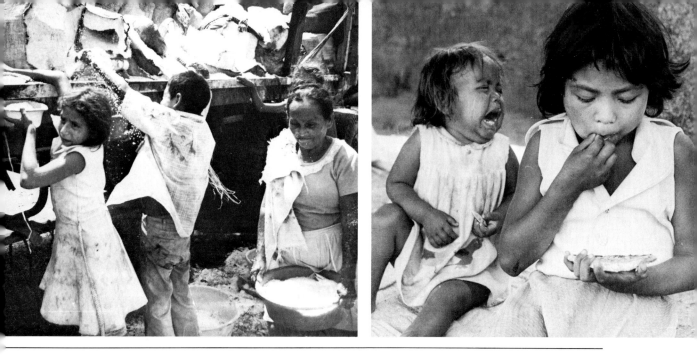

After tractor trailer rigs were stopped and set afire by guerrillas, refugees scavenged bowls of salt from the disabled trucks (left). A baby protests loudly (right) after her hungry older sister takes her food.

Salvador, many have gone to the cities. Others have been relocated in refugee camps throughout the country.

Less than one-fifth of the homeless in El Salvador live in refugee camps. Most of those in the camps are women, children, and elderly peasants fleeing the bombing and fighting around their villages. Life in the refugee camps offers no relief from hunger, sickness, and harassment. A lack of proper sanitation and inadequate nutrition contribute to numerous health problems such as malnutrition, skin diseases, diarrhea, parasites, and eye infections. Shortages of medical supplies and food are commonplace. Volunteers who attempt to alleviate the plight of refugees have been subject to constant harassment, torture, and murder.

REPOPULATION

Fed up with makeshift lives in refugee camps and urban slums, peasants have begun returning to live in their war-battered villages. Since 1985, thousands of Salvadoreans have left refugee camps in Honduras and El Salvador to return to some of the more than 160 abandoned towns and villages.

Many have come from the Mesa Grande refugee camp in Honduras, the largest in Central America. A barbed-wire fence encloses eleven thousand people in seven camps—they were originally built to hold two thousand. The refugees at Mesa Grande know they cannot wait for the war to end. By moving back to their land of origin, or as close by as possible, they have consciously decided to look ahead. They want to rebuild their lives and their nation, and to provide a better future for their families.

HEALTH

Hunger and malnutrition are the fate of an increasing number of Salvadoreans. The number of calories consumed by most Salvadoreans is the lowest in the Western Hemisphere. They do not eat enough food to meet minimal nutritional requirements.

Poor diets lead to serious health problems. At least 75 percent of children are malnourished. Hundreds of thousands of children may go blind because they do not get enough vitamin A.

In the film, *Witness to War: An American Doctor in El Salvador,* a peasant describes the anguish of watching his children die of malnutrition (seventy-one out of one thousand die before the age of one):

> I worked on the hacienda over there, and I
> would have to feed the dogs bowls of meat or

bowls of milk every morning, and I could never
put those on the table for my own children.
When my children were ill, they died with a nod
of sympathy from the landlord. But when those
dogs were ill, I took them to the veterinarian in
Suchitoto.
You will never understand violence or
nonviolence until you understand the violence
of the spirit that happens from watching your
children die of malnutrition.

The infant death rate is high, caused by several factors. These
include malnutrition, unsanitary waste disposal, substandard
housing, and polluted water. Only one-fourth of the population
has access to safe drinking water. Four out of five homes do not
have toilets. Diarrhea and pneumonia, not cancer or heart disease,
are the major causes of death. The average life expectancy in El
Salvador is sixty-four years, compared with seventy-four years in
the United States and France.

Many illnesses causing death could be prevented by the
provision of adequate health care and education. The few existing
rural hospitals do not have enough equipment, supplies, or staff to
be effective.

Two-thirds of El Salvador's hospital beds are in San Salvador,
which has only one-fourth of the nation's population. The
impoverished must resort to a poorly financed public health care
system that has suffered even more since the civil war began.
Numerous doctors and health workers have been specifically
targeted for repression by the government and the death squads.
As a result, many have fled the country.

Chapter 9

EDUCATION, RECREATION, AND CULTURE

Despite the political and economic turmoil, life goes on in this beautiful war-torn land. People go to school, play games and sports, go to movies, visit with friends, and celebrate special days.

EDUCATION

The law requires Salvadorean children to attend six years of primary school, beginning at age seven. Although most children start school, few finish more than three or four grades. Only a third of rural schools offer up to the fifth grade. Although school is free, many quit to help earn an income for the family. Eighty percent of children begin working between the ages of six and ten. As a result, only half of all Salvadoreans can read and write. Libraries and books of any kind are scarce.

El Salvador does not have enough schools, teachers, or books, especially in rural areas. Some students living in remote areas must walk for hours, often in the dark, to and from school.

The entrance to one of the buildings at the National University in San Salvador

Access to primary education is more widespread in urban areas, where students are more likely to stay in school. The wealthy and middle class can afford to send their children to private schools. Most are run by the Catholic church and have enough teachers and materials. The majority of students in private schools go on to secondary school and many continue to college. Many attend technical schools for careers in such fields as agriculture and engineering.

El Salvador has two universities: the National University of El Salvador and the Central American University of José Simeón Cañas (UCA). The National University was established in San Salvador in 1841. A law school and medical school were opened by 1853. By 1980 it had an enrollment of thirty thousand students and was viewed as a center for academic freedom and one of the last open forums for political dialogue.

Viewing the university's activities as "subversive," government troops invaded the National University on June 26, 1980. Twenty-two people were killed and an estimated $8 million in damage was done. Although the university was reopened in 1984, it is still associated with "subversion." Suspected professors continue to be targeted for repression, and "questionable" books have been removed from the library shelves.

The Central American University is a private, Jesuit-run university established in 1966. It originally was opened as a conservative alternative to the National University. After becoming involved with the activities of the popular church in the 1970s, it—and its faculty—were targeted for repression. One-third of the faculty has been threatened and forced to leave. It has been bombed numerous times and in 1989 six priests and two lay people were murdered, but the university has remained open.

The civil war and shrinking budgets for education have had a damaging effect on El Salvador's educational system. Between 1980 and 1982, more than 1,950 schools were closed. Many of the closed schools were converted to military barracks.

Teachers have suffered also as a result of the conflict. In 1965, they formed a union called ANDES. The government views teachers as a threat to the system. ANDES members have been targeted for repression and hundreds have been killed.

RECREATION AND LEISURE

Salvadoreans work very hard, but like people everywhere, they need to take time out to play and relax. Watching and playing sports is a favorite form of recreation. Popular sports include soccer, softball, baseball, and basketball.

Soccer, called *futbol* in Spanish, is El Salvador's national sport, and it is played with passion. Soccer stadiums are found in nearly

With a little imagination, everyday objects become playthings for Salvadorean children.

every city. From an early age, youngsters join school and neighborhood teams.

Most poor children have little time or energy for play. When they do, they play games that do not require much special equipment. Since there is little money for toys, children make do with whatever they find, such as tin cans, sticks, and rags.

Salvadorean children enjoy having their parents and grandparents tell them stories. Possibly because many Salvadoreans do not read or write, folktales and sayings are an important part of their culture. El Salvador has a long history of oral tradition. Many tales are derived from Indian legends about the creation of the world and human beings. Other stories revolve around the devil, a central character in many folktales, and the struggle between good and evil.

Movies and television are another popular form of recreation. Many of the movie theaters in San Salvador show foreign films with Spanish subtitles. Spanish-language movie theaters are more common in towns and villages.

Cojutepeque is known for its colorful market, a good place
for people to chat and catch up on the latest news.

Most people in the countryside do not own TVs, so they will
watch television at the village social club. The majority of shows
are from the United States and dubbed in Spanish. Many people
listen to the radio several hours a day for entertainment and
information.

Since there is little money for entertainment, visiting and
socializing are popular ways to relax and have fun. After the
evening meal, women may gather in friends' homes or on front
porches to talk. The men often meet for drinking and gambling.
Young people enjoy gathering in the plaza. Salvadoreans of all
ages enjoy having a party, especially when there is dancing.
Although rock and roll is sometimes played, most prefer
Salvadorean music. Popular dances include the *cúmbia, salsa,* and
ranchera.

On Sundays in the countryside, families often walk from their
villages to the nearest towns. They may go to the market and visit

Two views of Los Chorros, one of the country's most popular recreation parks

with friends in the plaza. Larger towns usually have one or more social clubs. The club, which may have a TV, juke box, and billiard table, serves as a locale for parties and socializing.

The wealthy and middle class have more time and money for leisure activities. They do much of their relaxing and socializing at elegant private clubs. At sports clubs, members are offered fishing, tennis, golf, horseback riding, and waterskiing. The social clubs can be very elaborate and may include a swimming pool, restaurant, bowling alley, billiard room, and ballroom.

April is a favorite month for outings to beaches, lakes, and other recreation spots. Throughout the country, the government has established a number of *turicentros*, or national recreation parks. One of the most beautiful and popular is Los Chorros, located near San Salvador. Waterfalls cascade through a misty gorge and into a series of pools, each overflowing into the next. Trails wind through exotic rain forests of ferns, vines, and tropical flowers.

*Events such as funerals (left) or religious celebrations (right),
break the routine of daily life and bring family and friends together.*

San Jacinto Teleférico is an amusement park and entertainment complex on a mountain above San Salvador. Swiss-made cable cars carry visitors to the top, where they enjoy rides, games, music concerts, and folk-dance concerts. In San Salvador, children enjoy going to the Parque Infantil (Children's Park). The park includes a roller-skating rink, amusement rides, and boat rides on a small pond.

HOLIDAYS AND CELEBRATIONS

The routine of daily life is often broken by special holidays and celebrations. Families and friends gather for weddings, birthdays, baptisms, and funerals. Most communities have their own carnivals and fiestas. These are celebrated with parades with colorful floats and costumes, fireworks, concerts, traditional folk dances, and athletic games. Vendors sell homemade food and handicrafts.

Left: Traditional candy vendors at the Virgin of Candelaria fiesta in Sonsonate
Right: Procession of the Palm Leaves, an Indian celebration

Most people get time off from work and school to observe official national holidays. The fifteenth of September is observed as Independence Day in El Salvador and the rest of Central America. A large military parade is held, and family outings and picnics are popular.

Because El Salvador is a Catholic nation, its most important holidays are religious in nature. The most colorful religious festival celebrates the Feast of the Holy Savior of the World. Also known as the National Celebration, the festival takes place during the first week of August. It honors the Holy Savior, who is patron of both San Salvador and the nation. People flock to the capital city to enjoy colorful processions, a large *feria* (fair), carnival rides, fireworks, soccer matches, and homemade foods.

The two other week-long celebrations are Holy Week and Christmas. During Christmas week, Salvadoreans decorate their homes and churches with elaborate indoor nativity scenes, called *nacimientos*. The scenes can take up an entire floor of a room and

105

may include farms, villages, and roads leading to the manger. Some families may decorate a Christmas tree as well.

Every town and city has its own patron saint, whose day is celebrated annually with a fiesta. The celebration helps keep local traditions alive. Festivities include parades, sports contests, dancing, food, flowers, fireworks, clowns, and music.

THE ARTS

Most notable developments in Salvadorean literature, painting, and performing arts have occurred in the twentieth century. Before the Spanish conquest, music and art played an important part in the social and religious lives of the Indians. One of the first priorities of the conquerors was to destroy Indian art and replace it with their own.

Nonetheless, Indian folklore and tradition have managed to find expression in music, drama, painting, and literature. With a renewed interest in their pre-Columbian roots, recent generations have been looking to their Indian past for artistic inspiration. As with other elements of Salvadorean culture, much of the arts in El Salvador are a blend of Spanish and Indian tradition.

Very little is known of pre-Columbian music. As there are no examples of written music, most of what is known is based on archaeological excavations and performances by contemporary Indian musical groups. Wind and percussion instruments were the most popular, and many are still used today. Single- and multi-toned whistles called *pitos* sound like flutes or piccolos. The *chirimía* has a reed mouthpiece and looks something like a clarinet.

The most common percussion instruments are the *tambor* and

Musicians entertaining with a pito and drum

tun. These large and small drums often accompany the pito and chirimía. The *marimba* is a xylophone made of wood. It originated in pre-Columbian Mexico and Guatemala, and was adopted as El Salvador's national instrument during the twentieth century.

María de Baratta, of mixed Spanish and Indian ancestry, is considered to be one of the country's leading contemporary composers. Her compositions helped to preserve Indian and regional music. Her ballet *Mosaico Cuscatleco* (Cuscatleco Mosaic) captures much of the Indian spirit.

Painting did not truly come of age in El Salvador until the twentieth century. Probably the best known of the country's painters is José Mejía Vides, who was born in 1903. With a simple style, his work vividly portrays life in the countryside. He has been called "The Painter of Panchimalco," because so many of his paintings depict this rural town. Julia Díaz is the country's best-known female painter. Her works have been shown in major cities worldwide.

Salvadorean art is often a unique blend of Spanish and Indian traditions.

Most Salvadorean literature has been written since independence. The nineteenth century spawned several important writers and philosophers. Juan José Cañas is considered El Salvador's most famous romantic poet. He also wrote the lyrics to the national anthem. Francisco Antonio Gavidia, born in 1864, was perhaps the most important intellectual and writer of his time. His poem, "To Central America," condemns tyranny and proclaims his faith in democracy. His work, which includes several plays, is still widely read.

Philosopher Alberto Masferrer was the first Central American writer to deal with social problems. He is most well known for his essays, although he wrote poetry and a novel. Masferrer believed all people have the right to have their basic needs met.

One of the most important literary figures of the twentieth century is Salvador Salazar Arrué, who uses the pen name of Salarué. The novelist, short story writer, and painter was born in

Sonsonate in 1899. The publication of his *Cuentos de Barro* (*Tales of Mud*) in 1934 marked the beginning of the modern Central American short story.

Two of El Salvador's most influential and controversial contemporary authors are Roque Dalton and Manlio Argueta. During his lifetime, revolutionary poet Roque Dalton was called El Salvador's greatest living poet and popular historian. Although Dalton was born into a wealthy family, he was critical of his country's social injustice. His concern for the suffering of the people is reflected in the line, "Altogether we have more death than they, but all together we have more life than they."

Dalton was arrested by government police and sentenced to be executed, but he escaped and lived in exile from 1960 to 1973. Upon returning he joined the guerrilla army, where he pressed for political as well as military solutions. A militaristic faction of the guerrilla leaders disagreed with his views and charged him with spying. In 1975 Roque Dalton was tried and executed by his critics. Among the volumes of his poetry and essays is a collection titled *Poemas Clandestinos* (*Clandestine Poems*). The first complete English translation of this collection was published in 1986.

Manlio Argueta is believed by many to be El Salvador's preeminent literary figure. The novelist and poet was born in San Miguel in 1935, coincidentally the same year as Dalton. In a compelling and vivid style, he writes of the daily life and struggles of the peasants. Two of his critically acclaimed novels, *One Day of Life* and *Cuzcatlán*, have been translated into English.

Argueta is a social activist and has been expelled from El Salvador four times for defending various democratic causes. He

Clockwise from bottom left: Women in the market at Cojutepeque, young boys in San Salvador, a mestizo couple from a rural area, women selling oranges to bus passengers, and shoe vendors taking a break

A view of San Salvador from the ruins at Tazumal

now lives in exile in Costa Rica. In his prologue to a book about daily life in the guerrilla-controlled department of Chalatenango, Argueta expresses his hope for the future:

> These Chalatenango peasants are the children
> and grandchildren of those who succumbed in
> the dye factories, in the sugar cane, coffee and
> cotton plantations. Yet they are not the same.
> Their new awareness is the dream come true.
> They are already half-way down the road: the
> remainder is held in the hands of the world's
> oppressors. This half is what yet remains to be
> fought for. Inhuman practices must be defeated.
> All of us must put our faith in humanity's own
> grandeur. The dream is one of coexistence,
> justice, and happiness. The dream lies within our
> grasp; it is awareness throughout the world which
> must play its part in helping us Salvadoreans
> see our dream come true.

A worker climbs a mountain of coffee beans to add the contents of his sack.

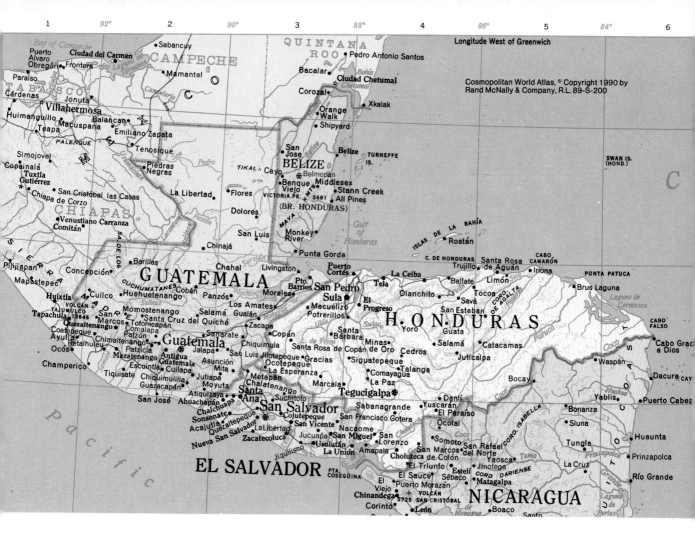

Longitude West of Greenwich

Cosmopolitan World Atlas, © Copyright 1990 by
Rand McNally & Company, R.L. 89-S-200

Map Key

			Metapan	C3
Acajutla	D3		Nueva San Salvador	D3
Ahuachapán	D3		Quezaltepeque	D3
Atiquizaya	D3		San Francisco Gotera	D3
Chalatenango	C3		San Miguel	D3
Chalchuapa	D3		San Salvador	D3
Cojutepeque	D3		San Vicente	D3
Jiquilisco	D3		Santa Ana	D3
Jucuapa	D3		Sonsonate	D3
La Libertad	D3		Suchitoto	D3
La Unión	D4		Usulután	D3
Lempa R. (river)	C3, D3		Zacatecoluca	D3

113

MINI-FACTS AT A GLANCE

GENERAL INFORMATION

Official Name: República de El Salvador (Republic of El Salvador)

Capital: San Salvador

Official Language: Spanish

Government: The government is a republic. In an election in 1982 a Constituent Assembly was chosen to draw up a new constitution and power was centered in a popularly elected 60-member National Assembly, elected for a three-year term. A president and vice-president are elected for five-year terms. The new constitution was adopted in December 1983. The country is divided into 14 departments.

National Song: "Saludemos la Patria Orgullosos" ("Let Us Proudly Hail the Fatherland")

Flag: The national flag consists of a white stripe between two horizontal blue stripes. The coat of arms is in the center of the white stripe.

Money: The colón, often called the peso, is a paper currency of 100 centavos. In the summer of 1989, 5.57 colóns equaled one U.S. dollar.

Weights and Measures: The metric system is the legal system, but some old Spanish measures also are used.

Population: 6,089,000 (1988 estimate): 43 percent urban, 57 percent rural

Cities:
San Salvador	452,614
Santa Ana	135,186
Mejicanos	88,989
San Miguel	86,722
Delgado	66,215
Soyapango	56,218

(Population based on 1984 official estimates.)

Religion: About 80 percent of the people are Roman Catholic. There is an archbishop in San Salvador and bishops in four other cities. There is complete separation of church and state and complete freedom of worship. About 5 to 10 percent of Salvadoreans belong to Protestant denominations; including Lutherans, Baptists, Mennonites, and several Pentecostal groups.

GEOGRAPHY

Highest point: Monte Cristo, 7,933 ft. (2,418 m) above sea level

Lowest point: Sea level

Coastline: 189 mi. (304 km) on the Pacific. El Salvador is the only Central American country without a Caribbean coastline.

Mountains: The country is divided into two highland mountain ranges and three lowland areas. The northern mountains, comprised of the Metapan and the Chalatenango chains, form the border with Honduras in the north.

Rivers: Of more than 300 rivers, only the Lempa is partly navigable. It rises in Guatemala, runs south into El Salvador, and eventually reaches the Pacific.

Climate: Located in the tropical zone, El Salvador has two distinct seasons: the dry season, from November to April, when light rains occur, and the wet season, from May to October, when the *temporales*, or heavy rains, fall. The coastal plain receives the heaviest rainfall. Temperatures vary with altitude; in general, the climate is warm, with an annual average temperature of 80° F. (26.7° C) and an average minimum of 64° F. (18° C). The average temperature in San Salvador is 72° F. (22° C) in January and 73° F. (23° C) in July.

Greatest Distances: North to south: 88 mi. (142 km)
East to west: 163 mi. (262 km)

Area: 8,124 sq. mi. (21,041 km²)

NATURE

Trees: Forests cover only about 7 percent of the land area. Indigenous trees include the mangrove, rubber, dogwood, mahogany, cedar, and walnut. Pine and oak are found in the northern mountainous region. Varieties of tropical fruit, numerous medicinal plants, and balsam grow in the country.

Animals: Jaguars, ocelots, and pumas still live in wilderness areas. Many species of monkey live in thickly wooded places.

Birds: Parrots (more than 34 species) and migratory birds are common. White owls, black vultures, hawks, pelicans, herons, swans, ducks, and geese are found in great variety.

Fish: Both freshwater and saltwater fish, turtles, iguanas, crocodiles, and alligators abound.

EVERYDAY LIFE

Food: Lunch, the largest meal of the day, may consist of soup, tortillas, rice, beans, cheese, or rarely, meat. A bread, fruits, vegetables, and sometimes fish are supplemented. A light supper consists of tortillas and red beans.

Housing: Most poor families rent one-room apartments in crowded, decaying buildings called *mesônes* that have no electricity or running water. Middle-class Salvadoreans live in row houses or comfortable apartments. Outside the villages are clusters of small homes, called *chozas*, made of woven branches and covered with mud. The very poor build shelters from any materials they can find.

Holidays

January 1, New Year's Day
May 1, Labor Day
First week in August, National Celebration
September 15, Independence Day
October 12, Columbus Day
November 2, All Souls' Day
November 5, First Call for Independence
December 25, Christmas Day

Culture: The culture of El Salvador has both Spanish and Indian elements. Old colonial festivals, such as the Day of the Indian and the Day of the Moors and Christians, are still celebrated by Indians in remote rural areas. A fair is held in San Salvador every August where native handicraft goods are sold. The National Museum at San Salvador has interesting old Indian relics, and about 20 mi. (32 km) from the capital there are some ancient Mayan ruins.

Juan José Cañas is considered El Salvador's most famous romantic poet. Alberto Masferrer is a contemporary writer well known for his essays dealing with social problems. Salvador Salazar Arrué, "Salarué," is a contemporary novelist, short-story writer, and painter. Two of El Salvador's most influential contemporary authors are Roque Dalton and Manlio Argueta.

Maria de Baratta is one of the country's leading contemporary composers.

José Majia Vides paints simple canvases depicting life in the countryside. Julia Díaz is the best-known female painter.

Sports and Recreation: Soccer, called *futbol* in Spanish, is El Salvador's national sport. Baseball and basketball also are popular. Most poor children, however, have little time or energy for play. Movies and television are another popular form of recreation. Most people do not have TVs, but watch them at their village social club. Dancing, visiting, and socializing are the usual ways to have fun. The middle and wealthy classes do much of their relaxing at elegant private clubs, where they play tennis and go fishing, waterskiing, and horseback riding.

Transportation: Until the late 1930s railroads provided the most modern transportation. Since then the government has built the most modern road network in Central America. The Inter-American Highway runs the length of the country. The most recently constructed Pacific Highway parallels the Inter-American Highway along the coast. Rail service is poor. A modern jet airport is located in San Salvador. About six airlines provide international service. The country's ports are La Unión, La Libertad, and Acajutla. Acajutla, which has been modernized, carries most of the traffic.

Communication: The press is reasonably free of government control, though it is owned by mostly conservative interests, and there is no opposition. Labor unions do advertise, however, and there is some criticism of the government. Two of the five television channels feature educational programs and are government operated. About sixty radio stations are licensed. The guerrillas operate two stations. Five newspapers range from conservative to ultraconservative.

Education: Primary education is compulsory, but only 65 percent of children of primary school age are actually enrolled. Illiteracy in rural areas is as high as 70 percent. The wealthy and middle class tend to send their children to Catholic schools. There are two universities: the National University of El Salvador, which includes a law school and a medical school, and the Central American University of José Simeón, a private, Jesuit-run university established in 1966.

Health and Welfare: The social-welfare system provides benefits to most employed persons for sickness, disability, and old age. However, many parts of the country experience poor health and sanitary conditions. Typhoid fever and dysentery are prevalent in rural areas. Malaria is prevalent in many areas. Trained medical personnel are lacking in many parts of the country. Diarrhea and pneumonia are the leading causes of death. Life expectancy is about 60 years. Hunger and malnutrition are increasingly serious. At least 75 percent of the children are malnourished and there is a high infant death rate. About two-thirds of the hospital beds are in San Salvador.

ECONOMY AND INDUSTRY

Principal Products:
Agriculture: Coffee, cotton, coconuts, sugarcane, cattle, chickens, pigs, lobster, shrimp
Manufacturing: Chemicals and fertilizers, cigarettes, cosmetics, cotton textiles, furniture, petroleum products, shoes
Mining: gold, gypsum, limestone, salt, silver

IMPORTANT DATES

1500 B.C.—Olmec civilization living in western region of today's El Salvador

A.D. 300-900—Maya civilization flourishes

1524—Pedro de Alvarado, sent from Mexico by Cortés, invades region now known as El Salvador

1528—Alvarado founds city of San Salvador

1539—San Salvador is transferred to its present site

1540—Spanish domination of El Salvador is complete

1551—Indian population reduced to about 60 thousand

late 1500s—Cacao becomes important export crop

1600s—Spanish culture predominates

1700s—Indigo, whose leaves were used for blue dye, becomes important export crop

1821—El Salvador declares its independence from Spain

1823—United Provinces of Central America is founded (a federation consisting of Guatemala, Honduras, El Salvador, Nicaragua, and Costa Rica) with Guatemala City as its capital

1824—Constitution adopted

1825—Manuel José Arce, a Liberal leader, is chosen first president of the United Provinces

1833—Anastasio Aquino leads first major Indian rebellion; is captured, tried, and executed

1840—Federation is dissolved; Francisco Malespin is chosen president

1840s—Wealth of El Salvador is controlled by the Catorce Grande, who also control the government

1841—El Salvador adopts constitution as independent nation

1845—Liberals regain control

1860-90—Half of El Salvador's land becomes private property owned by the wealthy

1871—Santiago Gonzáles assumes presidency

1876—Liberals return to power

1880—Conservatives return to power under Rafael Zaldivar who promulgates new constitution; coffee overtakes indigo as major export crop

1881—Land Reform Act deprives Indians of their common land

1886—New constitution is written, which provides for effective democratic process

1907—Trade union organizing among agricultural workers banned

1912—National Guard formed to control rural population and protect coffee plantations

1920—Workers begin organizing for change

1929—Stock market crashes

1930—Alberto Araujo elected president in first free elections

1930s—World coffee prices collapse and a peasant and farm worker movement rises

1931—General Maximiliano Hernández Martínez seizes power from Araujo

1932—Izalco Volcano erupts; Hernández Martínez unleashes a bloody assault against uprising encouraged by Augustín Farabundo Martí, known as *La Matanza* (The Massacre); Farabundo Martí is shot and his name erased from history

1935—Hernández Martínez reelected

1939—Hernández Martínez again reelected

1960s—Religious movement called "liberation theology" helps develop mass opposition groups

1961—Alliance for Progress formed; Central American Common Market established

1961-75—Landless peasants increase from 11 percent to 40 percent of the rural population; many peasants move to Honduras in hopes of a better life

1969—War breaks out between Honduras and El Salvador, three thousand killed

1970—Mass opposition groups, formed because of landlessness, unemployment, poverty, and overpopulation, cause civil disturbances such as strikes

1972—Christian Democrat José Napoleón Duarte is elected president, but the military cancels results; Duarte is arrested, tortured, and exiled to Venezuela

1977—Father Rutilio Grande, a member of the liberation theology, is assassinated

1979—Strikes paralyzing the economy and social unrest are widespread

1980—Archbishop Oscar Romero is assassinated while celebrating mass; civil war begins

1982—Alvaro Magaña, a banker, is named interim president

1983—New constitution is adopted

1984—Duarte, as a Christian Democratic candidate, is elected president

1985—Civil war escalates

1986—Earthquake kills 1,000 people

1988—Roberto D'Aubuissón's Nationalist Republican Alliance (ARENA) defeats the Christian Democrats

1989—Alfredo Cristiani wins elections and becomes president; Farabundo Marti National Liberation Front offer peace proposal; civil war continues

IMPORTANT PEOPLE

Pedro de Alvarado (c.1485-1541), one of Cortés's principal lieutenants

Enrique Alvarez Cordova (-1980), businessman, served in three governments; assassinated

Manlio Argueta (1935-   ), preeminent literary figure; writer of the daily life and struggles of the peasants; a social activist

Óscar Árias, president of Costa Rica, winner of 1987 Nobel Peace Prize

María de Baratta (1894-   ), leading contemporary composer; helped to preserve Indian and regional music

Juan José Cañas (1826-1918) famous romantic poet

Comandante Ana María (-1983), top guerrilla leader; founder of ANDES, a militant teachers' union

Hernán Cortés (1485-1547), Spanish conqueror of Mexico and Central America

Roque Dalton (1935-75), revolutionary poet and popular historian; critic of social injustice

Roberto D'Aubuissón (1944-   ), leader of ARENA party; right-wing extremist

Julia Díaz, best-known female painter

José Napoleón Duarte (1926-   ), mayor of San Salvador; elected president 1972; president of council 1980-82

Martín de Estete, leader of an invasion against the Lenca Indians

Augustín Farabundo Martí (-1932), son of wealthy landowner; helped found Central American Socialist party; hero of today's guerrilla army

Francisco Antonio Gavidia (1864-1955), playwright and poet

Santiago Gonzáles, assumed presidency of El Salvador in 1871

Father Rutilio Grande (-1977), a Salvadorean-born Jesuit who tried to organize the peasants; assassinated

Maximiliano Hernández Martínez (1882-1966), overthrew Alberto Araujo in 1931, first modern dictator

José Majía Vides (1903-   ), twentieth-century painter who portrayed life in the countryside

Ana Guadelupe Martínez, one of the top women leaders of the guerrilla army

Alberto Masferrer (1867-1932), philosopher, first Central American philosopher to deal with social problems

Carlos Humberto Romero (1924-   ), active in overthrow of government in July 1979

Óscar Arnulfo Romero (1917-80), Roman Catholic archbishop, one of the most beloved church leaders; his assassination touched off civil war

Salvador Salazar Arrué, "Salarué" (1899-1975), novelist, short-story writer, and painter

Mario Zamora (-1980), Christian Democrat, attorney general, murdered by death squad

Emiliano Zapata (1879-1919), Mexican revolutionary

Page numbers that appear in boldface type indicate illustrations

About the Author

Faren Maree Bachelis is a free-lance writer and editor of nonfiction books and articles for children and adults. She received her degree in anthropology at the University of California at Los Angeles, where she specialized in Mesoamerican and South American cultures.

Ms. Bachelis's credits include *The Central Americans, The Pelican Guide to Sacramento and the Gold Country,* and contributions to the *Lincoln Homework Encyclopedia* for Harcourt Brace Jovanovich. Her articles and essays have appeared in such newspapers as the *St. Louis Post-Dispatch,* the *Sacramento Bee,* and the *San Francisco Chronicle.*

Ms. Bachelis would like to thank her husband, Larry Bauman, and their daughter, Maia, for their patience and loving support.